TITCH - LIFE IN ONE SENTENCE

SHARON WAITE

GUTENBERG
Press

First Edition 2022 Fortis Publishing

ISBN-13: 978-1-913822-32-3

Fortis Publishing
Kemp House
160 City Road
London
EC1V 2NX

Acknowledgements

First, I would like to say without Ken Scott this book would not have made it this far, and thank you for bearing with me and guiding me along the way. A big thank you to my editor Joan for her understanding and patience and for taking the time to give me some precious honesty when needed.

Thank you to the few people who had to sit and have snippets of information relayed to them about whether I should put certain bits in the book and thank you to friends for the encouragement to actually publish. It's a scary but exciting decision to finally publish something that is so important to you personally and not knowing how it will be received. But the realisation is this is my story good or bad, and when I think about it, if it brings an ounce of help to somebody who has found themselves in the same situation as me, then it was all worth it!

About the Author

Sharon finally made the move to Cornwall after years of wishing, long dog walks on the beaches and cliff tops and lots of windy days. Long gone are the heels and suits which have been overtaken by a life of flip-flops and jeans.

Her peaceful time is in her garden talking to her chickens whilst dead heading her roses; a simple but peaceful existence after what seems so many different episodes in her life.

Her life has been full of lessons that she didn't know she had to learn, lessons that can be taught to others to make them appreciate the lives they have, and to show them that life is what you make of it not what you are given.

Sharon reminds us it's a beautiful world out there once you start realising it.

I would dedicate this book to my dear dad, who gave me the courage to conquer any battle and taught me all I know. He was my friend before he was my dad.

And to my children. The main reason I wrote this book was to give them an insight into life before them and to explain how the events of my life had an impact on all our lives and my acknowledgement of what they have been through which we have not had the courage to address.

Hopefully, this book will bring some closure on the past and is something they will be able to give to their children and say, 'Meet your Grandma!'

Part 1

THE EARLY DAYS

Well, where do I start? I suppose the beginning is as good a place as any.

New Addington – a place that many would say, 'Oh, don't go there – a rough place that.' The streets littered with broken-down cars, rows of local authority houses with gardens containing more toys than most playrooms, to me, were home. I am proud to say I was born and brought up there and still love it dearly to this day. This was where it all started, in a three-bedroom council house with no central heating, no phone and, when it was cold outside, the ice inside the window was thicker than on the outside and a method of entertainment was making shapes in the ice with our fingertips… thank God Dad had fixed the electricity meter so we could have two bars on instead of one – this is where it started, this was home

I knew every part of that house; every cracked window, every piece of missing wallpaper, the creak of every floorboard, the cupboard that didn't open unless you lifted it slightly and moved it to the left, every part of the garden and each plant in it. I loved it all – it was home.

Our family moved there in approximately 1960 when it was one of the first council houses built and a luxury for its time, a post-war prefab made of concrete that was only supposed to last for 20 years maximum to help with the shortage of housing following the bombings of Croydon and the baby boom that ensued after the war. It was a time when neighbours meant something and community spirit still existed, playing outside with no worries of paedophiles prowling the streets looking for unsuspecting victims – a time when the kids only went home when the streetlights came on or they were hungry, and each child had at least three 'aunties' in the vicinity who would offer them tea and a bed for the night should the need arise.

I don't really have many memories of my early family life; I have often tested myself on how much I remember. My earliest memory being one Christmas I had been given a pull-along toy, so I can only assume I was about two years old I know I was at an age where I had to tiptoe to reach the door handle, that's how small I was. It was a pull-along ladybird and when you pulled it; the wings flapped up. Oh, the delights of the simple things. I remember the snow being so bad we couldn't get out of the front door, the small pane of glass in the door was dark where the snow was covering it (and that was the top of the door!) I remember the black-outs of the 70s, us having a stock of candles in the kitchen just in case the electricity went and having to toast my bread on the open fire in the lounge or on the open coal burner in the kitchen that used to heat the water (must have been like an Aga but a council version). I remember dancing at school and being so proud that I had been chosen to be the one to wear bells on my hands and feet for Mayday, but I don't remember there being anyone to watch me. I don't remember the arguments, I don't remember any nasty feelings; I don't remember Mum leaving when I was about seven, taking my older sister with her. I only remember coming home from school one day and she wasn't there, but I was so engrossed with colouring that it didn't seem to matter. Dad was there and that was all that mattered to me. My two elder brothers were still at home but they were always out so they didn't count. I had my friends, my dad, and my Sindy dolls! It's at this point I really need to mention Jimbo. He was the love of my life and we were set to get married and live happily ever after; we had been inseparable since we were six months old. He lived next door but one to me. We walked to school together hand in hand every morning and afternoon without fail. When he moved to senior school, it all changed. The bubble burst – we had grown up! Anyway, back to the younger days.

From that point on, life changed. Dad became my world and, as far as I am aware, I became his. Dad woke me up in the morning with a cup of tea and a biscuit. Sometimes I went to school, sometimes I didn't. But Dad was always there when I came home. He would make dinner. We would do some homework together then I went out to play with my friends (there were plenty living down our road, a tree-lined avenue in a council estate) either climbing the street lamps or playing 40/40 till it was getting dark. Then I would wash, pyjamas on and watch some telly. It was time for bed and Dad would go off to work, leaving one of my brothers in charge of me.

Dad took on the night job of cold store-man for Ross Foods when Mum left so that he could be there for me during the day. When he went to work, either my brothers or a neighbour would look after me until Dad came back at four in the morning. I listened out for him and the familiar sounds when he came home; the whistling kettle, his teaspoon stirring the tea and the kitchen door creaking as he came up the stairs. I knew I was in for a cuppa with a biscuit. I would make out to be asleep until he put the cup down and the biscuit by the side.

It was only then that I would yawn and say, 'Thanks Dad.'

I settled, having had a dunk of my biscuit and a slurp of hot tea, back to sleep for a few hours before getting up for school. Looking back, I realise how hard it must have been for him. He was dealing with his grief at the split-up of his marriage and the thought of where his wife was and who was she with. Also, he was trying to cope with a seven-year-old girl and trying to keep everything as normal as possible plus trying to earn money as well to keep the roof over our heads. Unbelievable! I am glad I told him how proud I was of him and all that he had done for me, but I never understood what he had gone through until I was older and had that strange feeling of 'hindsight' I believe it's called.

Of course, as a child, I didn't see any of this; I was having a fantastic time playing with my friends and just being a child, it's a wonderful testament to how great a role my dad played. He kept this all hidden from me and made me feel loved and secure, never a worry about anything except whether my dog was following me all the way to school or not.

My biggest excitement was when Dad bought a caravanette – I thought it was the best thing ever, it was a big white van (maybe a Bedford) with windows on the side and a side door, but the best thing was it had stencils of Snow White & the Seven Dwarfs on it and some Disney characters I seem to remember. That now meant we could go on holiday! And I was right, we had some fantastic times in that caravan. Sometimes we took one of my friends with us, sometimes Dad's friend and his children came with us, but the best times of all were when we went on our own. It might have only been for a weekend or overnight, but it was great, and it seemed like we had summer holidays full of fun. That familiar memory of camping and boiling water on the gas stove to make a cuppa, my favourite place was the top bunk above the driver's cabin, that was my bed for the night, and I remember sleeping so peacefully there knowing I could sense my dad sitting around the open campfire or just sitting reading; peace.

Dad had suffered from a slipped disc; I think before Mum left. I never knew about it until one day I came home from school to find him on the floor. He couldn't move. I ran next door to get the neighbour until my brother came home. It turned out this had been going on for a while. He would collapse, unable to move, and then be like that for about seven days. Slowly, he moved around again. This would happen every few months and when it did, I didn't go to school but stayed at home with Dad. It felt right, but I think Dad got in trouble with the authorities for keeping me off school and I know my school work suffered because of it. But I didn't mind. I must have been about eight or nine years old.

I think it was because Dad felt guilty about my schooling that we started doing work at home – 'homework' I suppose you call it now! Dad bought a whole range of encyclopaedias which must have cost him a fortune. Every night we sat down and he set me a topic and I had to read up on it and write an essay and draw a picture.

Many years later, I found my essays in the attic. Dad had treasured each one of them. Little did I know at the time, but these essays were the mainstay of my education and were in fact going to give me better GCE results than many of my friends who attended full-time schooling! I still have the encyclopaedias sitting on top of my dresser. Some things you just can't move on from I guess, but they don't take up much room and they're not hurting anyone, so there they stay!

The only time I regretted not being at school as much as I should have been was when September came and the new school year started. Everyone seemed to know where their class was, who their friends were and where they were going – except me. I always avoided the first day back in September for this very reason, much easier to go back a few days later when everything had settled down and then you could ask what classes you were in. I swear to this day I spent half my time in classes I wasn't meant to be in. My pals at school knew what was happening at home, so I think they covered for me half the time and made my excuses. They are still my pals today and we meet up every few months for a curry and a giggle. Many people say how lucky we are to have each other. Believe me, we know how lucky we are. We have had some close shaves over the years, but we are here for each other and a phone call away, very lucky and treasured friends.

These were the days of playing British bulldog, looking forward to the weekend, starting with Saturday Morning Swap Shop on TV. Dad would get me a treat every Saturday. He would buy me two comics and a Mars Bar (I sliced it in a particular way, in half, then cut the caramel off in one section and chop the nougat into mouth-size sections to make it last). On Saturday afternoon, I had playtime with my friends who lived on the same street. It was my favourite day of the week and still is. I would come in for some dinner, then settle down to watch the Generation Game at night. Morecambe and Wise and Russell Harty followed on. Only people who were children in those days would understand that feeling. There was something magical in those years that I don't think later generations would understand. Life has changed so much and moved on to a world of technology.

'Give me back those days anytime,' I say.

Life carried on like this for what seemed a few years until Mum started making contact and wanted to see me. I remember Social Services talking to me, saying that my mum thought I didn't love her anymore because I wasn't visiting her. The truth of it is, I didn't want to. I was happy and busy playing at home; I didn't want to stop that. Talk about putting pressure on a young child. Those social workers sure know the right things to say. I guess that's the reason I haven't really got any time for social workers these days and I don't depend on what they say as it seems to me they don't really know what they're saying half the time.

As time went on, I saw Mum on the odd weekend. She was going out with somebody who drove a limousine, so I felt she was almost a celebrity. She lived in Croydon and went up to London at weekends. Her boyfriend was a bouncer at some of the clubs in London and knew all the right people (or seemed to). Going from my little house in New Addington to Croydon seemed like an adventure, just imagine, London.

Looking back now, I thought she would show me the good life that I wanted; much more than being stuck in New Addington for the rest of my life. As much as I loved it, I wanted more. There was a big wide world out there and I eventually bit the apple of temptation and moved to Croydon with my mum. I must have been about thirteen. I had just started my periods and didn't know what on earth was happening to me. Dad was of the old school and never really talked to me about sex education, women's things and all that, so I went.

Again, looking back, I cannot imagine how difficult it must have been for my dad to let me go, but I expect he wanted me to experience more than New Addington could offer and I love him for that.

* * *

Mum lived in a two-bedroom maisonette on an estate in West Croydon, with her partner, Tom. He was a chauffeur for the big names at the time and did security for concerts and events. Many a time I would go off up to London on a job with him in the back of the limo and push my way through the crowds to watch whichever band was playing. This was the first time I saw The Police and Sting, who later became my idol. They were little known around 1978/1979, doing small concerts at the London Palladium and suchlike. My autograph book filled rapidly with the likes of John Williams, who was a regular. It wasn't long before I started helping my mum in the cloakroom at The Embassy Club in London. I became a regular and, at the ripe age of fourteen, I knew everyone. It was a regular sighting in those days to see naked bodies walking about and men and women wearing very little while serving drinks and dancing, but I was in the cloakroom, taking in the coats and watching it from afar. I never realised how famous the club and the people were until I was much older. I enjoyed this time and am grateful for those experiences that many would only dream of.

My sister, who by now was twenty-two, called in regularly and sometimes stayed the night, bringing her carrier bags with her. She had met somebody at fifteen and gone off to live with him because she didn't like my mum's partner. Every time she had an argument with her boyfriend, she packed her clothes into carrier bags and went back to Mum. My sister was a bit of a rebel, drinking, smoking, not conforming to the rules. Her partner was ten years older than her and seemed exciting because he had a flashy sports car and took her to the best restaurants. But their relationship was, and always has been, unsettled. Despite this, they seemed to have held it together ever since. She is now 60 plus. (I have put that because she will have the hump if I tell her actual age!). Still married to her husband who she met all that time ago, resentful, and a bit of a rebel but has calmed down much more now. She has two lovely daughters whom she dotes on and sometimes I have to remind her she was a rebel once too when she has a moan about either of them.

Despite my sister moving out to go live with my mum, we have remained close, and I am very grateful for the relationship we have. I like to think I am her best friend, as she is mine. We spend time together, when possible, as we have done over the years, bringing up our children together. She has looked on me with a protective shadow. Perhaps she feels because I am her little sister, things have to remain the same. It used to annoy me when she would have an opinion on what was happening with my life, but again, in hindsight, I am grateful to have her in my life.

Mum broke up with her partner and started seeing several people, none of them worth their name on a piece of paper. I felt sorry for her because she was obviously looking for excitement and happiness. If only she had realised earlier that my dad was the best man she could ever have met. I don't think he ever stopped loving Mum and would have taken her back at the drop of a hat. They got on well later in life, but not to where a relationship was ever on the cards again.

This was not a good time in my memories, coming home from school in New Addington, putting the key in the door and hearing my mum inside with a stranger. I would have to wait outside the door until they had sorted themselves out - not the sort of thing you want to hear from your mum. I think this had a profound effect on my lack of respect for my mother, which continued through my entire life until my mum was old enough to need me and I was old enough to forgive.

I continued to see my dad regularly, and he even came down to Mum's for Christmas dinner and for card nights with my aunts and uncles. At one point, I even hoped they would get back together again so that we would all have a normal family life, but that was not to be.

My sister's boyfriend owned a petrol garage in Coulsdon and my mum started working there. I soon started dating the boy that worked there too. He was only a year older than me, and we became besotted with each other. Unfortunately, the first sexual encounter I had left me pregnant and without a clue about what was going on. I had never been told about contraceptives and my mum arranged an abortion. There was no real discussion about the options available to me. My boyfriend was distraught, but went along with it. From then on, I think our relationship was doomed. I made an easy recovery, but the memory was to stay with me forever and even now I think about how old the baby would have been had the pregnancy continued. I was still at school sitting my GCSEs. I remember having to leave the Art exam halfway through because I was feeling sick. I also remember the pencil drawing I had done of a puppet sitting on a chair… even half completed, I got an impressive B for it. If I had completed it I may have got an A, but who knows? For a brief spell, I went on to sixth form college. I wanted to be a journalist, but it cost too much to go to journalism college, and in those days, university was not an option. I doubt for one moment I would have been chosen coming from New Addington. I didn't know anybody who went on to university in those days. The clever ones went to college, and that was far from where I was.

I left school to start work in Coulsdon as a photographer and eventually more or less moved in with my boyfriend and his family for a while as they lived in Coulsdon. I returned to my mum's at Croydon and occasionally to Dad's at New Addington, which eventually became normal and my relationship fizzled out naturally. Helped along by the impact of the pregnancy and the resulting action, I felt I needed to find myself again. By now I had a social life with friends from work and started going out clubbing with a girl my age, Susan, who was doing deliveries at work. We seemed to be well matched for having fun and on the same wavelength. One night, she invited me to her brother Pete's girlfriend's 21st birthday party, which I happily went to. We had fun, and then we left, thinking no more of it.

The next day, I had a phone call at work. It was her brother Pete wanting to meet me for a drink! To be honest, I didn't even remember him from the night before, but obviously, he remembered me, and to cut a long story short, I agreed to go out with him. He said he had split from his girlfriend on the night of the party but I did not know that. I hadn't been focussed on him at all, but now it seemed a good idea and somewhere new to go.

We started seeing more of each other, going out regularly, along with his sister and his other brothers. It turned out he was one of fourteen children, believe it or not. To make it even stranger, when I told Mum about his family, she hit the roof and said I should stop seeing him. Apparently, their dad was the best man at my mum and dad's wedding all that time ago. My dad used to work with his dad – what a coincidence! Later, Mum told me it was because their dad didn't treat their mum very well, always down the pub and one for the ladies while she was at home with fourteen kids to look after. She didn't want that for me. Strange how fate happens no matter what warnings you have and how you think it's not going to happen to you. You never listen until after the event and when you look back, it hits you.

My friendship with his sister continued. She was seeing a guy who was a little strange but very good-looking. He wasn't the social kind, and it was odd how she had to be on call for him whenever he wanted her, but she never came out with him to parties, friend's houses or even just to the pub. Years later, we found out why.

He was the M4 rapist and after murdering a prostitute in London, he was recognised on Crimewatch and arrested, sentenced to spend the rest of his life in prison. It was a crazy time. The press followed us around and we used to go down the pub, pretending I was his sister to distract them from following her. Some years later, and shortly before he was due for release, they found him dead in his cell. It seemed that he had taken his own life. This devastated Susan and she has loved no one as much as she loved him, despite what he had done. I have remained friends with her over all these years, but this is something we rarely talk about; it was a strange time and not necessarily a good time.

My relationship with Pete became stronger and we got a flat together. I think mostly because he needed somewhere to live and I wanted to live away from my mum's but didn't want to go back to New Addington. It was time to move on. We rented an apartment in Croydon, a grotty, top floor, converted flat with a shared bathroom, but it was ours. In those days, we were happy. We both worked, we went down the pub socially with a good circle of friends and had a pleasant life, I was so much in love with him and thought he was in love with me. The future was looking promising.

We decided to look at buying somewhere together and, on a trip down to his sister's in Kent, we saw a new development in Orpington and took a look. It was a brand-new Barratt build and, in those days, a good option. We put a £50 deposit down and bought a one-bedroom maisonette that wasn't even built. It seemed like a good thing to do at the time.

Because we were saving up to move in, we went to my dad's and lived with him, thereby saving our rent money so that we could buy furniture. Everything was fine but it all seemed to turn a corner one day when Pete didn't come home at the usual time, just as I was starting to get worried, his van pulled up outside but he didn't get out. It was late at night and eventually, Dad and I went out to the van to find him sitting in the driver's seat asleep with vomit down the door and window. He was drunk.

From that point on, things changed. He became possessive, wanting to know where I was going and who I was going with. He came home at all times of day and night with no explanation. It embarrassed me that Dad was seeing him like this and couldn't wait for us to move out into our first home. I'm not sure if I just didn't want Dad to see what Pete had become or the fact that I was still with him, ridiculously thinking things would be any different in our own place.

For the first few years after we first moved in, things were good. It was exciting and fun. I got a job near to where we lived. He was still self-employed working at Croydon. My social life had stopped, but his had continued at Croydon. I was ready to settle down. He wasn't. His drinking was getting worse and with that came the inevitable. He would look for somebody to blame, and that person was me. Several times I had to make excuses for a black eye, a bruised arm or a leg, but I forgave and made excuses. Was it that I didn't want to accept what was happening or was I scared to admit I failed in a relationship? Was I blaming myself for driving him to it? He had said it was always my fault. Had I pushed him to this?

One night, he was arrested driving home, and the police charged him with drunk driving; he lost his driving licence. As he was self-employed, he needed his van and tools to continue working and asked me to give up my work to drive him. Rightly, or wrongly, I refused. I had my career and didn't want to give mine up because he had been caught drink driving. His sister's friend needed a job, so he employed her to drive him around. I should have known really what would happen with the way he had become.

One evening, we were having friends over for dinner. He had rung to say he was going to be late. The friends turned up, and we had dinner without him. Then they left. The night came and not a word. I did the usual ring round of hospitals to make sure he had not been involved in an accident, and then, in the early hours, I rang his parents to see if they had been informed of anything. Nobody had heard from him, not even his sister Susan. I had sat up all night, worried sick about what might have happened. The next day, I drove over to his parents to retrace his steps and find out what had happened. It was a complete mystery. Nobody knew anything. I went down to the local pub, which I knew he used, and asked around but got nowhere. Nobody had seen him, no accidents had been reported. He had vanished, and it seemed I was the only one looking for him. I just couldn't work it out. At home, I sat by the phone day after day, knowing that any minute I was going to face the fact that something awful had happened. Then the doorbell rang.

It was a face I didn't know, a man. He asked me if I was looking for Pete. He knew where Pete was and gave me an address at Croydon that I should check out. I didn't even consider not going, as I was desperate to see him, make sure he was okay. I drove to the address and, as I pulled up outside, another car pulled up and he got out and went to the door of the house and was met by a young blonde girl who wrapped her arms around him and kissed him. Oh my God! My world fell apart. I started my car up and wanted to ram it into the first car I saw. I drove and drove, and, to this day, I still don't know where I went, devastated and sobbing all the way. The face at the door informing me of his whereabouts was the girl's boyfriend, and the girl was the friend of Susan who Pete had employed to drive him. Apparently, they had run away to Wales for a week of lust and now they had come back and were living at this address in Croydon.

The days/weeks/months following just blurred into one another. It devastated me even though I knew things had been getting worse; I didn't want to accept them. Eventually, I accepted another job at the Holiday Inn Hotel at Croydon and my social life was looking healthy again. I was still living in the flat and travelling to Croydon for work. He rang me at work to let me know he was at the flat taking his stuff and she was there with him. I was furious. I couldn't cope with the emotional stress and feeling that the flat was not my home anymore and moved back to Dad. The flat sold, and it was all over. Time to start again, or so I thought. We sold the flat and made a small profit. We both came out with about £10,000, which in those days was a good profit. I never saw Pete again.

* * *

My life picked up, my career changed, and I started working for Vodafone at Croydon (London Car Telephones) earning a good salary, mixing with interesting people and having a good life living at my dad's. My career hit a new high when I became PA to the utterly charming and good-looking. Customer Services Director. It wasn't long before I was enchanted by his character and flattered by his attention. We started a romance. I knew he was married, but he assured me they were separated and the fact that he had been married twice before did not ring any alarm bells. I was totally enjoying myself, my career was looking good, and I was travelling with the company. I was driving my choice of car, either a Porsche, a Mercedes or the meanest looking Ford Sierra Cosworth 4 x 4 (my preferred choice). My lifestyle boosted my confidence, and I wished things would never end. Unfortunately, end it did in the most drastic of circumstances. His two-year-old son was diagnosed with a terminal stomach disease and died in hospital.

At the funeral, no one was aware of our relationship as we had been very discreet, but he constantly held my hand as if he knew he would have to let go one day. That was the last I ever saw of him. He left work and disappeared. I carried on, but it soon became clear that, although he suffered under tragic circumstances, he had left work dubiously and left lots of questions unanswered. Because I was his PA, I was questioned too, although I knew nothing about the business side of what was going on. I think they suspected I knew more than I did. It was time to look for another job.

About six months later, driving through Addiscombe, I saw Pete sitting outside a pub on his own and, ridiculously, I stopped. How fate could have changed my life if I had kept driving, I do not know, but there we go.

He said he was on his own and all the old charm came spilling out. We talked about going for a drink, whether it was because I was vulnerable or whether I hoped he had changed, but I said yes. We met up, went through old times, and then started seeing each other again. He was living at a bedsit in Addiscombe and invited me over. Even after all these years I still cannot explain why I did not see through this to the man he was and walk away.

He stayed with me, and I stayed with him, then we saw a house for sale and went for it, make or break. We could put a small deposit down because of the profit from the sale of our first flat. The house needed so much work doing to it, but it was lovely with a little garden too. We had big plans for what we were going to do and how it was going to cost. I think looking back, the house was up for £73,000, which seemed massive at the time, but it was a good buy and we started work on it. The house was right by the park entrance and we had lovely neighbours. We only had second-hand furniture, but it was ours. It wasn't until later that I discovered he was still living with the girl he had run away with when I started seeing him again! Now that I am typing this, I want to slap my head and tell myself to keep running as far away as possible.

My life had taken a new turn, I applied for a dream job with the BBC; it was only a trainee post, but it was a start and I was based at Television Centre in Shepherds Bush. It was a nightmare to get to, but I didn't care; I was so proud of myself for moving forward, aiming for higher, and hitting it. I was floating and nothing else seemed to matter. Two hours was a long distance to travel morning and evening just to get to work, but at my lunchtime, I could go over to the recording studios and watch Top of the Pops or Blue Peter being recorded so I was happy and all I had to do was keep remembering that.

After moving into the house, I realised Pete's drinking had got worse and his temper had grown. He became so possessive of me, he wouldn't let me wear tights or stockings to work. I could not put make-up on and I never went out with him to the pub. Our lives grew separate. We were constantly up and down. One weekend I would run away to my dad's but then return after a few days. On one occasion, things got terrible, and I didn't return for a while. I was scared, but I still had spirit in me and I was trying to make a life for myself away from this person; I moved my things out. I even started dating someone else trying to forget about him, but all he needed to do was snap his fingers and I would go running back. This time when I ran back, I discovered I was pregnant. Things got a little more serious than concerning myself about my life. I knew now there was another life to worry about that was far more important.

When I told him about the pregnancy, he never reacted. We went through the motions, telling the family, moving my things back into the house, and making plans. I knew my life would change from that moment and that was what I was here for.

We had the usual doctor's appointment. She warned me I was likely having a large baby and sent me down to the hospital for the normal scan. Pete came with me, but there was something different. When the doctor scanned, she turned to look at her notes and then announced, 'It's twins!' Now that was a shock.

Throughout my pregnancy, life was good. Pete was a changed person, caring and loving. He was working hard on the house to make sure it was okay for when the children came along and he was working hard, earning money to pay for everything. The children were born by Caesarean Section on 18th July 1991, one girl and one boy, and in that split second in the hospital when I realised I had given birth to the two most beautiful people I had ever seen; I knew that my life was worth living and if I achieved nothing else; it didn't matter.

For the first year of being parents, the glow of happiness continued. I was so in love with Pete again and grateful for these lives we had produced, but slowly, things changed. Why I will never know. Perhaps it was my fault for focusing on the children, but change they did.

Pete went back to being possessive, jealous, almost hating me for the person I was. He went to work in the morning and came home after closing time every night, the worse for drink and if I dared to confront him about it, he would blame me for winding him up and then headbutt me, hit me or throw me down. Any form of aggression towards me and my confidence was destroyed. I was already scared of what he would do to me if I tried to leave, and this reinforced it. I should be a better person, a better mother. I should do as he tells me and clean the house, have his favourite food ready whenever he comes home, and not ask questions about where he had been or who he had been with.

I guess you could say I became one of those wives everyone asks why they stay with their partners when they are like that, and even I cannot understand it. Why did I stay for so long in such fear and living a lie? To all his family and friends, he was a good sport, a laugh with his mates down the pub, a provider for his children, and a good family man. He joined in birthday parties for the children every year in the garden. We invited our families and friends.

Each time I thought, Perhaps we will be okay now.

That would last for a week and then we returned to being the same people we had become. The truth of it was, the mortgage wasn't being paid; I was shoplifting cheese just to feed the children who hardly ever saw him. I had to make sure I was in bed pretending to be asleep before he came home at midnight or else…

I could tell of the times when the police were called. When I had to make out to my dad that I had tripped up because I had a black eye. Where I told work that I was out cycling and had fallen off my bike which was why I had an egg-sized lump on the front of my head, not where it had been smashed against the kitchen taps because I had not cooked his pork chops the way he liked them! If it was worth telling of the arguments where I used to have to steer him into a room where there was nothing precious, if I thought he was going to get angry. He used to take it out on my possessions and smash them up. Anything that I loved, he would destroy.

I could mention the times when I caught him with other women or when I picked the children up from school and, as we walked past the pub, his van was outside. I could see him in there drinking and knew he would be there till after closing time. The sadness that I used to feel not only for my life, but that of my children but also for Pete, wasting his life because he was not happy.

Life continued. The children started school, and I got myself a part-time job with a building company to give me some independence and to help pay bills and buy food.

It all came to the crunch when the children were six years old. It was Christmas Eve, and he came home from work about lunchtime and announced he was going to Croydon to get

Christmas presents for the kids. He returned home about five o'clock with bags of stuff; all for him. Clothes for going out that night. As usual, he spent the evening down at the local, only returning home about two o'clock on Christmas morning. He went to bed. I had to get dressed up as Santa and wrap up the few presents I had bought for them, so they at least had something.

We had arranged for my family to come for Christmas dinner at our house that year and I was busy in the kitchen preparing dinner when I heard him get up, have a shower, come down and go out. No word about Happy Christmas to me or the children. The family came for dinner. He came home about four in the afternoon, drunk, fell asleep and went to bed. I decided there and then I would never spend another Christmas with this man, and I never did.

It came to a point shortly after where he had done the usual, gone to work, followed by the pub, and then came home at eleven in the evening. I could tell by the swing and smash of the gate that he had the hump, so I pretended to be asleep. I heard him coming up the stairs and felt my heart beating so hard yet trying to remain calm so he didn't realise I was awake. He came into the bedroom and started shouting about his dinner, which I ignored and carried on pretending to be asleep. He shouted in my ear and I knew I had to get away from him otherwise I would get head-butted, so I got out the other side of the bed, ran from the bedroom into the smallest room and hid behind the bed. Ridiculous, I know to think that would protect me. He stormed in and tipped the bed upside down on top of me. I screamed. The children woke and screamed. I went into their room to comfort them, but he followed me. I think it was the look of horror on my daughter's face that said it all and, thankfully, he walked out. I stayed in the bedroom with them and eventually we all fell asleep.

It took me a few months to get myself strong enough to leave. We rowed, we cried. He left, he came back, but eventually, I knew the only way I could leave was to do it without him knowing. He had told me often enough that he would make sure if he couldn't have me, then nobody else could, and I honestly thought he would carry out his word.

The house was in negative equity and where we had not kept up the mortgage payments in full; they were threatening repossession. There was nothing left to fight for. I looked for a rental property.

I found one for a fair price, far enough away to make a completely new start. One guy that I worked with part-time, Mark, said he would come and look at it with me. I had told him the situation, and he said he would help however he could. I looked at the house and agreed there and then that was the one for me. It looked beautiful, green striped lawn, on the edge of the forest within a small village with its own cricket pitch. How idyllic! At first, I thought, Surely this cannot be the rented house I applied for? But it was, and I had no hesitation in accepting.

I got the strength to tell my dad what had been going on with Pete and what he had become, something that I had told no one before. I was ashamed to have let him treat me like that. Leaving was against my dad's wishes; I think because he didn't want to see my family split up the way his was. Eventually, he came round and helped move me in. Pete had gone to his parents for a few days on the advice of the police to cool down not knowing we were leaving. The children and I moved out. They were allowed one bag of toys each. We took the dog and the cats and left with as much as I could take in a small Austin Metro; we were stacked to the roof!

Amazingly, we settled in overnight, and I knew when I moved in that I never wanted to move from that house. It brought with it such peace and felt like home as soon as I stepped through the door. The children hadn't asked once why they weren't going home or where Daddy was. They were excited, running around the garden having fun. The person inside me that had been held down for fourteen years held her head up and breathed.

Over the next few days, Mark rang to make sure I was okay and invited us out. We went to Eynsford where the children played in the river. The park or the beach were places where the children ran around. Our new life was good, and we got used to Mark coming round for dinner or to walk with us over to the woods.

After a while, I contacted Pete so that he could see the children. We planned for me to take them to my mum's and he went there to see them. He was still furious, and I did not trust him to be alone with them at this stage. Eventually, things settled down and he would have them for the day, once every few weeks.

When I moved into the house, I had to seek income support to help me pay the rent on the property, as I was not working and had no means of support. As it was a completely new area, the children had to go to a new school. I looked for work locally. Obviously, I didn't know anyone in this area but my dad came over regularly to sit in the garden with me. Dad met Mark and they became good friends. It wasn't long before Mark became more than a friend to both me and the children.

* * *

It was quite a shock when I found I was expecting another child, but not a surprise. I had always wanted another baby, but knew I could not have brought another child into the situation I had been in. Here it was different. It was peaceful and happy. However, it came as a shock to Mark, who thought he would never have a child, and to his mum, who thought she would never have a grandchild by her only son.

Mark moved in. He had asked me to marry him, and my dad gave us his blessing. The children saw more of Mark than they ever did of their own father. Suddenly, I was asking myself why I hadn't moved out sooner. My life had changed in such a short period. I was where I had always wanted to be, out in the country, with a man that seemed to like the same things I did. I could be myself. I didn't have to worry about wearing makeup, having my hair done or wearing the wrong type of clothes. The children could play out on the green and have friends round for tea without worrying about their dad coming home drunk and embarrassing them. It was a lot to take in!

Our first Christmas came and went, January arrived and with it came the birth of my third child, Jacob, a beautiful baby boy who looked like Dad, and a dad that was so proud; a little scared but unbelievably proud. Mark's mum was delighted with Jacob and Mark. She was grateful that we had given her a beautiful grandson that she absolutely adored. She visited us every week, bringing down something nice for the twins. I don't think she realised but to this day they remember her because she always knew what they liked and attempted to bring them a treat every week. She was a good woman.

As I didn't know anyone in the local area, I went to the local Toddler Group and soon discovered that it needed somebody to run it, so I accepted the voluntary role and thoroughly enjoyed it. This meant I could make friends with all new mums in the area and also my baby had other babies to play with. These were good times.

Life took a different turn. My sister and I used to take the children away for a break whenever we could. A stay in a caravan or a cottage, anywhere we could have fun and let the kids all just run together. We had some great times and loved to go down to Poole in Dorset to a caravan site, Rockley Park. One day, Mum approached both of us and said rather than leaving us money when she died, she wanted to buy something that we would get pleasure from and gave us the choice, the money or a caravan. We had had such a good time in the caravan, that was what we chose. We took Mum down to Rockley to do a deal with a brand-new caravan. It was perfect, and the kids loved it. Every moment we could get we would jump in the car and set off to the caravan for the weekend.

We have wonderful memories from the caravan days. The kids playing out on scooters, going off on an adventure, bunking down together in the rooms at night, usually with me on the sofa. I loved it as much as they did, me and my sister sitting on the balcony putting the world to rights, knowing the kids were safely tucked up in bed. These were special times, never to be forgotten. We rented the caravan out when we weren't using it to help pay the yearly site fees, which I used to organise. We had regular customers who always treated the caravan well and looked after it as we did.

Life seemed too good to be true. The children had adapted to their new way of life and they had a beautiful baby brother. They had both taken to Mark as a stepdad. We had a garden party every summer when it was the twins' birthday and barbeques in the garden with singing and dancing in the kitchen. We didn't have much, but we had love, and everything was just perfect. The Famous Five we called ourselves. In June of that year, we took the family out to Groomsbridge Place and had a great day but on the way home Jacob's leg developed a nasty rash. We got home and immediately realised it wasn't a normal rash and would not disappear under a glass. We rushed him to hospital where they instantly put him on an antibiotic drip and 24-hour supervision. They suspected meningitis. I rang Dad from the hospital and asked him to go home to look after the twins, but he reacted strangely. Something was wrong. He said he hadn't felt too well. I assured him I would get someone else over and ring him as soon as we heard anything. I didn't realise but Dad had just had his first heart attack.

Jacob pulled through the next day. The medication was working, and the rash disappeared. The doctor said it may have been an allergy to pigs. He had sat on a pig at Groomsbridge Place! Whatever it was, they had caught it in time, and all was fine. They sent us packing.

When we got home, I left Mark with the children and went up to Dad. He was still feeling poorly. Then my sister and my dad's friend, Uncle Charlie appeared. Ignoring his disapproval, we accompanied him to the hospital where he underwent tests. They put him on an ECG machine to monitor his heart and kept him in overnight. We said our goodbyes and came away, knowing he was in the best hands.

The next day I went to the hospital with Jacob and as we were sitting there, I could tell Dad was uncomfortable. Then the machines started reacting, and the nurses rushed in. Dad was having another heart attack.. I sat with him and held his hand while the staff attached wires and monitors to him, trying to lift his spirits and assure him he would be okay. Believe it or not, he got through it. The doctors gave us the talk about how the first attack had damaged his heart and they needed to do a test where they put dye through the heart to see how much damage it had sustained, but there was a risk of a stroke. I chatted with Dad, but he refused the test. He had an overwhelming feeling that he was going to have a stroke and end up a cripple, completely dependent on his children, which he didn't want. He was 67 years old and very active.

Over the next few days, Dad's strength built up and each day, he would save some of his dinner for Jacob. We would sit for a couple of hours chatting, trying to tell Dad to be quiet because when he spoke it would put a strain on the heart, but he wouldn't listen. My sister and I took it in turns to be there, me in the morning, her in the afternoon, and then I went again in the evening. After approximately a week, Dad discharged himself against the doctor's wishes. They wanted him to undergo further tests to see and repair any damage, but Dad was stubborn and just wanted to go home, so home he went.

Our lives changed that day. When Dad was at home, he could no longer eat what he wanted. No more crisps, no more fat, lots of vegetables and fruit, and under no circumstances was he to exert himself, for a while at least. Dad was doing really well, but was grumpy. He didn't like putting anyone out of their way, didn't like the thought that he couldn't do things himself, but I kept telling him it was only for now; that when he was stronger, he would do things again, but at that moment, he had to sit and watch TV while I made dinner!

Bless him, he did as he was told until one morning before I had got there; he got a bill through the post and walked round to the post office to pay it. By the time I arrived, he had had another heart attack and was struggling to breathe. I didn't realise what had happened and just kept asking someone to get help but he was angry at talk of an ambulance. He just needed to get his breath. He had to keep sitting on the floor to get his breath. He would not hear of an ambulance. He said he wanted to be at home and rest. I was on my own with Jacob, who luckily was asleep. I got Dad up to bed, tucked him in, and made him a cup of tea. I sat with him for a while and told him I loved him and stroked his hand. He rested and said he felt the best he had in a long time, and then he dozed off.

Jacob woke up. I went home intending to return once Jacob had been fed and was asleep again, but about thirty minutes later, the phone rang. It was Uncle Charlie. He was at Dad's but there was no answer at the door. I told Charlie that Dad was sleeping but I would come and meet him outside.

If I am honest with myself, I knew then that Dad had gone. In the car on the way there, I wondered how I would react? What am I going to do without him? How am I going to tell the children? He was their role model, the only solid thing they had ever known. There wasn't a day that passed that they didn't see him. A million and more questions were running through my head, but then I would snap out of it and tell myself not to be so stupid – it would all be okay. Mark drove me to Dad's, and I let myself in with the key, calling up that it was only me. As I went up the stairs, I felt such a sense of peace when I walked into Dad. I crouched down beside the bed and cuddled him. He had only just passed over. I called out to Charlie and then it goes blank for a while. The sadness takes my memory away like a protective cover. I think

Mark rang my sister and brothers and I sat with Dad. He looked like he was just asleep, but his eyes were slightly open, but he didn't look like he was in pain. He was peaceful and hopefully still having a pleasant dream, remembering his life and now reuniting with his mum, dad and family. That's the way I like to think it is.

Dad died at approximately eight in the evening but my brothers, my sister and I spent the evening sitting in the garden, taking turns to be with Dad until the morning came and then we called the doctor. When the ambulance arrived to take Dad to rest, the birds stopped singing, and the garden was silenced. When Dad left the house, the birds started singing again.

Everyone said I was the strongest following the loss of Dad, the youngest of the family was becoming the rock of the family, but grief has stayed with me for many years and the feeling of loss has played a significant part in many decisions I have had to make in my life. I cannot bear loss or say goodbye to anyone or anything, it must be see you later and even that brings a tear to my eye.

I know I suffered depression in the immediate months following his passing. If it had not been for the children who needed me, I know I would not be here now. Dad's words, from his last known will and testament, repeat in my head. 'Please don't be sad for too long. Continue with your lives. Be happy.'

All I want to do is scream, 'How can I be happy without you?'

I refused to leave Dad's house to the council. He had been paying rent for years rather than buying it, therefore they were trying to claim it back so that they could put somebody in the home that had been ours for forty years. I continued to go up there every day to feed the cats and make sure all was okay. In some deep part of me, it felt like Dad was still there too and I would sit in his front room and make two cups of tea, one for me and one for him, but the house was so quiet. Looking back, I think this was where my issue with not letting go may have started. The feeling of losing everything and everyone has had such an impact on my life and has been an excellent lesson. We all need to move on at some point, to let go of the past and embrace the future.

Eventually, the council won and reclaimed the house. I tried to save as much as I could of our memories, but they called in the workers and ripped the place apart. I was a mess and couldn't face the fact that I would never set foot inside again, so it was better to walk away. They put in a new kitchen (when Dad had suffered the original kitchen all that time despite requests to renew), completely rewired and shipped in another family that completely trashed it.

Even to this day, if I could ever purchase it from the council, I would and then turn it back to how it was all those years ago. That's if I had my way, which thankfully, I don't.

In the meantime, back at home, I was getting myself into more and more of a depression, cutting myself off from friends and not caring about anything or anyone. All I kept doing was getting in my car and driving up past the house, sometimes parking outside and just watching to see who lived there. Sometimes looking at the bedroom windows and remembering the times we had spent doing the garden when Dad sat on the front doorstep whilst I dug over the flower beds. Then I would drive off crying. The time had been a blur for me. I woke up every day, got the children to school, cooked, and breathed. This felt like it was the most I could do just to exist. Looking back, I believe I was in a deep depression that I couldn't get a hold of.

Everything passed me by without a care, or so I thought.

Shortly after losing my family home, the owners of the rental property I had moved into announced that they wanted to sell it and they were giving me one month's notice to vacate. It was all too much; Mark and I sat down and did our sums. Based on the value of the property, the mortgage repayments were the same as the rental payments. We purchased the property so that we could stay there. I had not told the council that Mark had moved in; I was still claiming help with the rent. I wasn't working as I had been pregnant, with no way of supporting myself, so at the time I couldn't see any option. Mark was giving me £50 per week towards the food and bills, but he knew I was also claiming help. It's no excuse, but I wasn't even thinking about the consequences.

* * *

Luckily, the property that I had fled from previously had not been repossessed as threatened and Pete had taken in a lodger to help pay the mortgage. I found out the property had been sold. Mark had been on the ball and told me to make my claim as it had been in joint ownership, and I was due my share of any profit. Pete had not told the solicitor that I was no longer present and was intending to keep the proceeds of the sale. I contacted the solicitor and registered my interest. There was a small profit, enough to put down a deposit on our present house and enable us to get the mortgage. As I wasn't working, Mark put the mortgage in his name and drew up a Deed of Trust for my fifty percent of the house. Only one small but major problem, I did not tell the Income Support people that first, he was living with me, and second, he had bought the property and I continued to receive housing benefits and income support.

Six months later, in 2001, I was investigated and told that I would be charged with fraud. As soon as I received the letter, I immediately signed off benefits, went and got a full-time job, and opened my eyes for the first time in a couple of years, life goes on, so now I had to get on with it.

It all seemed like a nightmare that I just couldn't wake up from. A cloud hung over me permanently, no matter what I was doing. I was progressing in my job as PA to a Director of a local housebuilder because of the experience I had of working in the same industry before. Although I had been out of the role for a while, it all came back to me. I earned money to pay my way and juggled the children with after-school clubs and a childminder for Jacob. We were establishing an honest system of taking care of everyone and all the bills. Mark was working permanently, having started up a new business with his working partner. We were both pushing forwards trying to put right what we had done wrong.

I was called into the Council Benefits Office for a taped interview, which I obviously went to. At the time, I saw no need to take a solicitor. After all, I was now working and trying to get on with life again. I walked away and heard no more for approximately four months until seven o'clock one morning. There was a knock at the front door. Mark answered and called me down. The room was full of armed police officers who had come for both me and Mark. The children were asleep upstairs and unaware of this. They told us we were both under arrest for making a false statement and that we were going to be taken away to be questioned. If I had no one to look after the children, they would be taken into care. I woke the children, got them dressed for school and tried to carry on as normal. The policewoman followed me as I dressed and got the children ready. All the while, they searched the house for evidence. My two older children were aware of what was going on. I explained it to them as briefly as I could without alarming them and sent them off to school. My youngest son came with me to my mum's, and I asked her to look after him until I got back, whenever that was to be. This was one of my worst memories of all time.

From then on, we were under a constant threat of being charged. It was like a big grey cloud of doubt hanging over my head. How would I repay the amount owed? Perhaps they would give me community service, but at no point were we prepared for what would happen. Eventually, I was sent notification of a date of the court hearing some three years after being investigated.

On the day of the hearing, I had already gone out and bought a little cuddly toy for each of the kids and written to them in the worst-case scenario and hid it in the under-stairs cupboard. I tried to talk to Mark about what would he do if the worst happened, but he wouldn't listen, kept stopping me and saying that it would be okay, but it wasn't. I guess he may have been thinking that if he didn't acknowledge it, it wouldn't happen.

Even though I was no longer claiming, and hadn't been since 2001, the Department for Work and Pensions did not give up. They kept alive the charge on me for fraudulently claiming income support and housing benefit back to when I first moved into the property. They threw everything at me, even down to free school dinners for the children. They left nothing out and would not take on board any appeal. Consequently, they charged me at Guildford Crown Court with fraud and making a false statement on six counts and sentenced me to nine months' imprisonment. They had racked up the debt to be in excess of £90,000. To this day, I do not know how they came to that figure, but apparently, this was why they pushed for a custodial sentence.

In the dock, I was shaking continuously. It soon became clear that they intended to lock me up from the start with no hope of community service, and this became clear when I heard the charges they were throwing at me. It was at that moment that my vision stopped focusing on where I was and what was happening. I remember Mark jumping up and pleading with them because of the children, but it all became a blur, as though I was watching it from somewhere else and it wasn't happening to me. All the words they spoke echoed in my head like a distant echo and seemed to last forever. They took me away instantly to a holding room. I was empty, void of all emotion. With a passing glimpse of Mark standing in the gallery and not knowing when I would next see my children, they took me out the back door. It was 21st July 2004.

Part 2

THE INSIDE LIFE

I took the following from my diary entries from my time spent inside, followed by my memory of my feelings at that time. My twins were thirteen and Jacob was four, just about to start school. The first part in *italics* is my actual diary entry for the day.

BRONZEFIELD

Wednesday 21st July 2004

'What a day, it all seems a bit of a blur, a living nightmare. I just cannot believe this is all happening to me, nor can everyone that I speak to. All the guards are just shocked that I've been sent here for what I done, they all seem to look at me and realise the kind of person I am because they are so nice to me, but that doesn't change the fact that I am here for 4½ months, hopefully shorter if I get 'tagging'! I've cried so much

today that I have such a splitting headache that I am grateful to be locked in this cell on my own tonight.'

This is the diary entry for my first day. The staff kindly gave me some paper to write on as it took a while for me to get some personal items into the prison. They took me from the court room to the holding cells and left me there for a few hours until they had enough people to fill up a prison van. I was left with my own thoughts and feelings; what a terrible thing! I remember the guard as I was walking from the dock. He kept saying, 'Don't worry, you will be out for Christmas.' Those words actually comforted me in some form, as I was swamped with emotion and all I could think about was the children. It seemed to take ages to arrive at Bronzefield. It felt like the other side of the world, whereas in reality, I believe it's up near Heathrow Airport. I remember looking out of the van window and all I could see were the trees and the people walking by on the side of the road. I remember seeing conkers on the trees and thinking the kids would like to knock them off the tree to take to school. But that journey seemed to take the longest time. I had been crying so much that I couldn't think straight anymore. I couldn't even think of the children and what they were about to find out. It was just too painful.

Once at Bronzefield, they take all your details, photo, issue you with a prison number, awful olivegreen tracksuit and plastic trainers, toothbrush, toothpaste, soap, pyjamas, and then strip search you. By that time, your dignity has gone and you couldn't care less where they poke or prod you because your pride is out the window at that stage. They then put you into another holding cell with everyone else, and this is your first taste of the people you will spend the term with. Luckily, I had already been assured by the guards at the court that I wouldn't be spending Christmas inside. I would be out by then, which, believe it or not, made me feel better. I couldn't stand the thought of being away from the children for Christmas.

They then led us to the central office, where the inmates are allocated where they will go to, A, B, C or D wing. A is for drug users who are on methadone now; pretty grim in there I can tell you, B is for general cases awaiting trial or sentence, C is for hardened criminals awaiting trial, sentence or allocation to another prison, D is empty. We were standing in the middle, waiting for them to decide on our wings.

Through the bars of A, were a group of girls calling me over. I looked different from the others because I was wearing a suit. Trying to impress the judges that I was a professional person worked against me in the end as everyone thought I was Miss Goody Two Shoes and they had something to prove. The feeling got the worst of me and I couldn't control myself anymore; I broke down and cried. Luckily, one guard on duty saw the situation, realised I wasn't handling it well and took me aside. He obviously saw this was my first time, and he explained the procedures step by step. What would be expected of me, what to expect of others, who to stay clear of, what not to do, and basically said that if ever I needed to talk, he was there any time night or day. Looking back, I am so grateful to that guy. He made me feel I wasn't alone. He gave me the phone and told me to make a call and left me alone to ring home. Unfortunately, I cannot remember what I said or who I spoke to. It's all a blur now. Then he took me to my allocated cell, which was in B. I was given a single cell. They led me there, shut the door and left me to it. I was so exhausted I just wanted to sleep and escape from this nightmare.

Thursday 22nd July 2004

'Feel devastated today, lots of tears again, don't want to go out of my cell at all. Mark came to visit this afternoon which was lovely but I so wanted to go home with him.'

When I woke up that morning, I had been dreaming that I was at home and there was some noise in the background, which I thought was the kids. It was only when I came to and opened my eyes, that I realised it was the commotion going on outside my cell with the other girls getting their breakfast that had disturbed me. I got up and into my green tracksuit, but I couldn't face going out and seeing all the inmates, so I sat in my room looking out the window. The smell of the room was nasty. I looked around, scared to go to the toilet in case someone came in. I sat there until eventually one of the staff knocked on the door. It was Carl, the guy from the day before. He sat down and told me I have to pull myself together and go out there and face them. The longer I left it, the worse it would be for me. The other inmates would think I felt too good to mix with them and start shouting and banging on my door. I was terrified at what was out there, but I knew it had to be done.

I pulled myself up and opened my door. To my surprise, nobody looked up. They carried on as they were, queuing up for breakfast and sitting down to have their cups of tea. I quietly joined the queue, got some toast and tea, and sat down. A few of the mates glanced over at me and smiled. With their smiles, I felt a wall had been knocked down. I smiled back. I had established a link and the feeling of dread disappeared.

Mark came to visit in the afternoon, which was good and bad at the same time. He told me how badly the kids had taken it and he looked dreadful. It was so nice to see him, but it made me feel even worse when he went. I felt it would be easier to have no contact on the outside while I had to do this time.

Friday 23rd July 2004

'Tried to get my pill today from the doctor just to keep my periods regular, but still nothing, after queuing up for one hour - all the other girls there needed methadone. I'm too scared to tell them mine was for the contraceptive pill!

Had induction finally this afternoon. The system here is ridiculous, you are supposed to have induction when you first get here so that you know what you can and can't do, etc, then I was told I couldn't yet use the phone, then I got really upset, they just don't care, I think eventually they were concerned about my state of mind so I was granted an emergency call to call home. I was so stressed by then that I just cried which was not what I wanted. It was lovely to speak to everyone - gave me hope, upsetting too, but in a nice way. Jacob kept asking what day I was coming home - I would sell my soul to be home now.'

Because of the layout of the cells, with an open plan toilet immediately inside the door, I couldn't bear the thought of having a period in there and the other girls seeing me do my private business. I thought it would be easier to stay on the pill. That way, I would not have a period at all whilst I was in there, so I went to the doctor. That opened my eyes. I was queuing up for the doctor with the other girls getting methadone. When my name was called, I went up to the window to ask for the contraceptive pill. The doctor replied he didn't have any but did I want methadone instead? They seemed to give it out like painkillers in there, whether or not you want it. No wonder there is such a drug problem.

Saturday 24th July 2004

'12.45pm. I have just had lunch which consisted of one ham roll, soup and wet salad, and that was the good choice, the alternative was a suspicious looking beef curry, what looked like a regurgitated turkey curry and plain stodgy rice - for a change!!

Now we're on 'lock in', hopefully this afternoon will be gym for 2 hours, that will help to pass the time. I've only just managed to get some of my own clothes from reception, (it makes you feel more human to get out of prison issue green tracksuits), Mark brought my belongings in with him on Thursday along with letters from home, some photos of the children which I am so desperate for. It feels so lonely here on your own and somehow it seems to make a difference when you are looking at the people you love. It's so nice to hear from home, to know they are there gives me hope. I can't even begin to explain the desperation that you feel in here just to have normality - home.

Still haven't heard anything from them about working etc, I have applied for everything I think - just to try and make the day go quicker.

I went outside into the garden earlier, it was so sunny. I sat on the grass and looked up to the sky and thought about what the children would be doing now. Then I thought that if I look only at the sky I could be anywhere in the world – I imagined that we were all at the Wittering's beach, the noise was of the children playing in the sand and the gentle breeze from the sea. It worked for a while but then my eyes opened and saw the walls and hear the other prisoners all talking. Then it was time to come in. It was nice for a while.

Beginning to spend a little more time outside my cell now chatting to the other girls, made a few friends, one of them Melissa, a 23-year-old Irish girl, also a mum of 3, in here for conspiracy to fraudulent marriage – she's only on remand and hasn't even been sentenced yet and she has already been here for 3 months! Hopefully by the time her case comes to court she should walk free from the court as any custodial sentence imposed would already have been served. That poor girl and her poor children, she has no partner and her ex is looking after her children, he is refusing access for her mum to see them even, she has to deal with all that and being in here not being able to do anything about it. It makes me feel how lucky that I am that I have my family at home all pulling together. Melissa is on constant suicide watch because she keeps trying to cut herself.

Then there is Christina, a 30-year-old German Lorry Driver who is completely innocent in my eyes. She talks some English but struggles to communicate with the other girls. Again, she is on remand and came in a few days before me. She picked up a load in France to deliver to Folkestone, unbeknown to her the load contained 4 tons of tobacco of which she had no idea. They are trying to charge her with smuggling. The poor girl hasn't even rung home yet to tell her Mum & Dad where she is, they still think she is on the road! The worst thing is that the date for the courts to hear her case is some 3 months away - how ridiculous is that!

Most of the girls I say hello to but that is all - I tend to keep myself to myself and spend a lot of time in my cell on my own just reading. Still waiting for writing paper to even be able to write a letter home. It seems to take everyone 2 days to do anything in here.

Actually received my pin number for the telephone so I may be able to ring home later today.'

Sunday 25th July 2004

'Went to the chapel this morning - what an experience that was - it was a gospel chapel - the type where they all get up clapping and singing, it was actually quite emotional. There was a row of Nigerians at the front who started chanting which was a bit scary but it was okay. Spent the afternoon walking round the garden and chatting with the girls. At lock up at lunchtime I sat and wrote my letters and put up all my photos on the wall using toothpaste - feels like home now that I can look at everyone looking at me.

Then about 4pm they announced I was moving - just like that, along with 4 other girls but not any of my friends - I felt a bit strange about moving but I was okay, until it come to the move and I just burst into tears - that fear came back again of not knowing anyone, being scared of where you are going to, scared of the girls and what they might be like - all very unsettling.

Anyway, its now 8.40 and we are locked in our new rooms, I've unpacked and I've put my photos back up on the wall - tomorrow is another day and I will start again. I will still see my friends when its 'Association' (time outside). I feel sorrier for Melissa because she was really depressed and she seemed to come out of it whilst I was there - I hope she will be okay.

Won't be able to ring home until at least Wednesday when I get more credit on my phone. The children will be down the caravan with my mum and sister apparently. I am so lucky to have my home and my family, once I get through this I know there is no problem resettling and I will try to carry on as normal as if nothing happened - its just that our lives stopped for 4 months!

After speaking to other girls here, most of them do not know what they are going to do when they get out - they have no home to go to and their children have been put in care! I know I am very lucky to have what I have and if my only lesson learned from this experience is that, then I feel I have achieved.

I find it very hard to even think about home because I just cant go down that thought - it is too painful and I know if I get depressed about this whole situation I will not be able to get out of it, so best not to go there in the first place, I look at my photos, have a little cry, kiss them all goodnight and concentrate on something else.

I went to get my pill again from the doctor and guess what - he still hasn't got the prescription - 4 days now - but did offer me something else instead! Didn't care what, he just said "is there something else I can give you instead?" with a tub of methadone in one hand would you believe - I think he was expecting me to take methadone because that's what everyone else was having - I told him I wasn't going to put anything in my body that wasn't' prescribed as I actually cared about my body. That's the big problem here they think you are like everyone else - palm them off with methadone regardless of what their problem is - unbelievable!'

Wednesday 28th July 2004

'Well, would you believe it, I have been here one week now, only another 9 to go!

Had my chat with the relocation lady yesterday, she seems to think I am an ideal candidate for 'open prison'. Apparently there is one at Sutton Park so that would make it easier for people to get to and also it may mean that I could possibly see the children during my time, she was even talking about home visits at weekends - oh heaven!!

I got my canteen today so I have a bottle of water now, some phone credit and a piece of chocolate - Yes!

All the girls here have taken to calling me 'Angel', it's because my one white top that I have has Angel printed on the front of it, the name seems to have stuck which is fine. One of the 'top' girls had to write a legal letter to her solicitor to appeal her case so she gave it to me and we wrote it professionally together, that seems to have given me a bit of 'street cred', I now seem to have become accepted as one of the girls and they leave me alone.

Went over to the other block today to check on Melissa, I haven't seen her since I moved out - she was in her cell and cut up all her arms - I gave her such a rollicking, told her how stupid she had been and remember them 3 little beautiful children that are out there waiting for her etc etc. There was lots of tears and talking, I recognised the signs of despair in Melissa, the despair that I once felt when you lose control of all your muscles and you cant stop the shaking, of your legs, your arms, your chin, it makes it easier for me to cope with when I feel I have helped somebody else. I think they will try and move her over to my block so that she at least has somebody she feels she can talk to - she is constantly on suicide watch at the moment where they check her every 30 minutes. They will probably move her over just as I get moved out!

Hopefully I should get a job tomorrow - if not, I'm going to take over Nicky's cleaning job, she goes home tomorrow. I forgot to say, Nicky is the image of my cousin Sandra and even talks like her. To make the situation even more scary, she has a tattoo on her arm of the name Gemma, that's the name of Sandra's daughter and apparently the name of Nicky's daughter too - how peculiar!

Phoned Mark tonight - it was nice to speak to him - he put my mind at rest because I got a letter last night from my sister saying they were all going to Marbella - I was happy for them all that they were getting on but deep down I wanted to say "wait for me - please" but Mark said that nobody is going anywhere till I come home - that made me feel heaps better. It will be better for Mark once they all go back to school, routine will be easier and it will be even nearer to me coming home.

Mark said it will be in the papers tomorrow - oh god, oh well, get on with it, that's my attitude at the moment - bring it on.

Not much else I can do here. I know one thing, out of all this badness can only come one thing - goodness. That is my thought for the day that keeps me going. Goodnight xx'

Thursday 29th July 2004

'Haven't written all day, now its 10.50 and I am sitting on my bed in tears - but not for the reason you expect, I have just finished a book called 'The Gift' by Mia Dolan. Her experiences have touched my very heart and she is the first person to have put in writing what I have been feeling for over 5 years now, since Dad died. When I get out, one of the first things I must do is contact her at www.miadolanltd.com, apparently she lives near Leysdown in Kent.

There is a reason why this is happening in my life and I want to know what it is. I need to know what this is all about now, no more assuming, I need some answers - good or bad.'

Just for information only. Looking back, Mia Dolan was a real comfort to my soul during this time, and in fact, I thought about a time when I was younger. I was going out with my sister and her friends one evening and I was driving. The friends had made an appointment to have a reading with this lady at her house, which I seem to remember was in the Isle of Dogs direction. One by one, they had their reading and I was sitting waiting for them so we could go on to the wine bar or wherever. Anyway, the last one came out and this lady looked at me and said, "I've been waiting for you." I didn't have an appointment but I followed her and she gave me a reading and a prediction of various stages in my life that I was going through. So far, one by one, they have all come true. There are a few things still to happen, but we will see if they do. The reason I am saying this is that I think this lady was in fact, Mia Dolan.

Friday 30th July 2004

'Bad day today - big time!

Started doing the cleaning on the wing (better than just sitting around) and I was mopping upstairs - one of the 'girls' was laying on her bed and she called me to mop her room! (We are all responsible for our own rooms), I told her I was mopping the landing and she had to come down and get the cell mop if she wanted to do her cell, she said her legs hurt! I just ignored her and carried on and she came out calling me a slapper, a slag, bitch - the lot. I just put the mop away and went downstairs. I made a cup of tea and sat for a chat with Debbie and the other girls, but she wouldn't leave it, she was hanging over the balcony shouting names at me, threatening to 'get me later in the showers', I was trying my best to ignore it but I could feel my bones shaking inside my skin, one of the guards came over and Debbie told me to tell what had happened, so I started to explain and then just collapsed - I could feel all my blood inside my whole body popping and I know that I had to try to control it or I would lose it completely. Luckily one of the guards, Christian took me to my room and calmed me down, I was shaking all over and couldn't breathe. He called in a couple of witnesses and reported the woman, who left me alone after that - I keep seeing her look at me and say something but I am just ignoring her. Made me feel that way the whole day though.

Mum and my sister came to visit today which was nice - I wanted to hug them for ever - it just all feels so unfair. I stuffed myself with chocolate and orange fanta while they were here and didn't stop talking - I don't think they got a word in edgeways. So much to talk about but nothing really to say.

Its nice to hear that everything at home is as normal as it can be - I don't know how I will ever repay everyone for all they have done. Had a lovely letter from Mark today - I love and miss him so much, I know that when I come out of this hell hole I am going to marry that fat bloke whether he likes it or not - we are all going to be one family in every sense of the word!

I've told my sister to write again about them sending me on to an open prison - her letters seem to have an effect and actually get somebody listening.'

Saturday 31st July 2004

'Not much exciting happening today, two other girls nearly kicked off at breakfast - the 'witch' seems to be forgetting our confrontation thank god!

They locked us up at lunchtime and two of the guards come and took me to an interview room and asked me if she was giving me any more problems – it's nice to know they are looking out for me.

Spent the afternoon over the gym and then sitting out in the garden, finally got some colour on my legs.

Rang home tonight at 6.30 but the kids were still at my sister's house. Spoke to Mark, he obviously got word of what had happened yesterday and was worried. I told him I was okay now – there's no point him worrying too! He told me I've only got 58 days left - sounds better than 8 weeks eh! As long as I just keep my head down, do work, do all the activities I can, the time will go - I can do this - I have to do this, I am determined to make it through this, I will not end my days in this hell hole - not for anyone.

I'm missing the children badly, my brain seems to be in hibernation, it's strange, I can't seem to go beyond thinking about the kids - I think it's my brain's way of protecting itself from so much pain. I look forward to speaking to everyone at home - but then when I do I get so upset, especially when Jacob asks what day I will be coming home - never mind what month! One day sooner.

58 Days to go.'

Sunday 1st August 2004

'Today is a milestone believe it or not, it's now August, soon be September. Nearly 2 weeks I've done now.

Not much happened today. Went to church again this morning, which I actually do enjoy. Sat in the garden this afternoon with Melissa and Debbie and Rachel and then went to the gym this afternoon to try and work off some of these potatoes!

Rang home tonight and spoke to all the kids and Mark and I only had £1.20 credit left. Jacob asked if I was coming home when he wakes up, I said not quite, then he said "when I wake up after I wake up?" I just said soon, as soon as I can.

They call us criminals but a true crime is keeping a mum away from her babies - perhaps we're not the criminals after all!

I think things will all be changed when I finally get out, I think the children will have grown up and forgotten me and they will hate me for not being there for them - then I have to keep telling myself that its only 10 weeks, they will still remember me and love me. One thing I do know for sure, when I get home I will never ever be parted from my family again - no matter what!'

Monday 2nd August 2004

'Bit of a confusing day today - the allocation guy came round today and saw me and Debbie and basically said that there is no place for an open prison except if we are prepared to go to Lancashire - which we are most definitely not! Therefore he is going to have to send us to another closed prison. Debbie is off to Cookham Wood in Rochester tomorrow. I've said there is no way I am going to Holloway or Downe View, therefore the only option is Cookham Wood or wait for an open place - but I don't know yet what is happening.

Had a giggle with the girls today, Jenni locked me in my cell because she was jealous that I had got 3 letters so when she let me out, I flicked her bad neck - we did giggle. Jen is a 38 year old heroin addict whose finally managed to kick her habit, she is one of the kindest girls I have ever met in here, but boy does she have a wicked temper! For some reason I feel very safe being her friend.....

One of the other girls Lisa then locked in one of the other girls as a giggle (Lisa is 8 months pregnant, due out in January but will probably have the first baby born on the New Baby Unit), unfortunately the other girl didn't see the funny side of it and got the hump, but we all had a giggle anyway. Sometimes when we have a good day its like being in a girls boarding school, all of us giggling, singing, dancing, shouting to each other 'good night John Boy' from our cells, but then on other days...'

Thursday 5th August 2004

'God the day is going slow today – it's raining with thunder and lightning, everyone in here is angry today - so frustrated at being locked up all day and some of the things they have asked the guards to do have not been done which does not help the situation. I fell asleep this afternoon for 3 hours - probably won't sleep tonight now. There's gym to look forward to tonight so hopefully I can wear myself out before bedtime.

Never mind, I've still got lovely thoughts of my visit yesterday with Mark to keep me going. It was lovely to see him - I came back to the cell with a very warm loved feeling - I am so very proud of him.

Done the puzzle last night in my cell from the library - garden birds, nice puzzle, sat up till 11pm doing it - two bits missing!

I can tell we are all adjusting now - me and Mark only had a little tear yesterday, he said he felt better now he had seen me - his mind is at rest because I am as settled in here as I can be - I hope they don't move me now. I am trying desperately to keep doing puzzles, jigsaws, read books, newspapers etc, anything to keep my brain active, it would be very easy in here to sit in the corner rocking, there is just nothing to do and nowhere to go. We've had no going outside for 2 days now because of the rain - the other girls got the monopoly out today and Kim was trying to recruit people to play with her, Kim is the meanest looking person here but she is actually quite gentle sometimes but with a psychotic temper so I decided not to play just in case she lost!'

Friday 6th August 2004

'Went over the library this morning and hid reading the newspapers - until they realised I was missing and then brought me back!

Jan came round and confirmed that I have been allocated a place at East Sutton Park (open prison) but they are just awaiting my pre-convictions before they transfer me.

Done the bins at lunchtime and one of the guards told me that Rose West is coming into here - and that Tracey bird who done the road rage killing, their prison is closing down apparently and they will be putting them here until they move them to another prison. Well of course this is now the talk of the prison and everyone is gossiping about it.

Not sure how I feel about moving - probably quite good as it means I may get home visits to see the children but on the other side of it, I am settled here and know all the girls etc, I just want this all to be over with - it has been an experience, not one that I ever want to repeat but I hope that it will be one that I am grateful for.

Rang home tonight - Mark told me that he got the news today about the move and is very excited - then I rang my sister, the children are all having a sleepover there tonight - she said the same thing, apparently the Governor rang her today to tell her.

When I do leave here, I will send them a thank you card, especially for Kristian, Jennifer, Sally, Rachel, Tine in Reception and of course, Les. They have all made my time here easier to accept because of the people that they are - I have certainly had a huge lifetime experience here.

Tara came back from hospital today - she has been miscarrying since she came in here - nearly 3 weeks!! They took her for a scan yesterday and there was still some foetus left in her so she has had to go and have a termination. She is in her cell now (9.30pm) being sick and crying - I know we are all prisoners but she shouldn't be in there alone at a time like this.

Had to zip my mouth today - they moved five new prisoners in and they were all travellers, sitting round the tables, no teeth, holes in their arms from injecting, nits in their hair and they were all bragging about the 'creep-ins' that they do - burglaries while the people are asleep upstairs, boasting about the amount of money they get at the loss of other people - I really had to hold myself back - these are a different life form - they do not understand right from wrong and the word 'morals' does not exist in their life.

One girl of 29 has been in and out of prison for 11 years and has 2 children. I asked her why she does it, why not get a job and earn money like other people, her answer was that 'her quality of life is high, she wants the best - new car, designer clothes, holidays, house etc'. She stated that when she gets out there is a new car waiting for her, in her eyes its worth spending time away from her family and children in exchange for nice possessions.

My point was proved when she showed us a picture of her children's first communion - I asked where she was in the picture - 'in here' was her reply - I think she knew how I felt when I looked at her - my head was thinking, 'you missed that - for this shit.'

No respect, no value for life, no thought for them poor people that she has thieved from and what they are or have gone through - just so she can have a new car. I really need to button my mouth - perhaps this will be my task for this weekend.'

Sunday 8th August 2004

'Well, there we go, the weekend has gone as quick as it came. Went to church this morning, came back for lunch and then went to the gym this afternoon, sat out for an hour with the girls and then tea and lock up.

Tomorrow will be strange, there are a lot of people moving off tomorrow, the atmosphere here will change, especially with the new girls that have moved on, the majority of them are methadone girls - they all stick together.

In a way, it will be a good thing to move out, hopefully next week. Wrote to Jackie to thank her for the cards.'

Monday 9th August 2004

'Oh its 8pm and I have had enough today - I wish they could just give me an injection and wake up on September 29th, some days this place really gets to you, one minute they tell you your release date is... then they say they can't let you go because their paperwork is behind.

On top of it all we have just had a 'dealer' put on the wing and she is 'offering' all the girls crack cocaine - the temptation for most of them is just too much - makes me so angry, they've been through so much to detox and sort their lives out and some little scum smuggles some in, god knows how, and all their hard work and suffering is wasted.

I just want to be moved now and serve my time the best way I can. Still haven't heard anything. I think I'm just pissed off in here, nothing to do all day except sit round the table bitching – it's really getting to me now. Glad for lock up today.'

Tuesday 10th August 2004

'Well, today wasn't really any better than yesterday. Woken up at 6.30am, they shipped out Penny and Lynette to Moreton Hall in Lancashire. Lynette is due to go home next Thursday - crazy eh!

The day didn't get much better, more new people moved in, more drugs, somebody was banging the cell door all night because they had no methadone - apparently 'clucking' is what they call it in here.

Lisa had a drug's test this morning for her application to the Mother & Baby Unit, we all know that will be positive because of yesterday, so now she probably won't get into the Mother & Baby Unit and as soon as she gives birth the baby will be sent home to Nanny rather than being with Mummy - all for a quick fix.

A couple of people have had their 'tag' confirmed - go home this week. I eventually got my date for being moved through - next Tuesday 17th August - a whole week away. I rang Mark tonight and told him, I got so upset, I've just had enough, sometimes you realise where you are and what you are doing and its all too much. Spoke to the children but it's hard to hear them on the phone with everyone screaming and shouting. Mark said he's coming down tomorrow – that's something to look forward to.

I tried to busy myself cleaning up the store cupboard and then cleaning out the empty cells and putting new sheets/towels etc in for the next person. They all think it's hilarious the way I do it, I put shampoo, soap, toothpaste etc on top of the towels and fold back the sheets - it looks like a hotel room when I've finished. All the guards chat to me like one of the staff, they all know I'm more than happy to help out just to be doing something.

Got a letter from Debbie today, she's been moved to Cookham Wood – doesn't like it at all and is trying to move to East Sutton Park - might see her when I go there - hope so.

For some reason today/tonight I cant seem to get the children out of my mind - I feel like I'm no longer part of my family - the feeling that they will have forgotten me by the time I come out is so overwhelming, the pain inside is like a grieving pain – it's a mixture between a sick feeling and an actual pain inside your heart like a big hole.

Every night I seem to be dreaming of the children and in the dreams I have lost them or they go missing and I am out of reach and cannot save them. I just have to hold on, one more week and I'm nearly half way, I keep thinking I will make it up to them when I'm out - I am not going anywhere for ages - I need quality time at home with my family to get back some of what I have lost, if that is possible.'

Wednesday 11th August 2004

'3 Weeks today.

Oh what a day - woken up at 4.30 by Amanda, screaming and shouting 'call an ambulance', went running to the flap and saw her being dragged up the stairs by 4 guards.

The day progressed - at 11am Kemmie (Head of Residents) came into my cell and said that as I was due to go to open prison next week, they had decided I might as well get on my way today - and I could be given a Release on Temporary License to Mark so he could drive me to the other prison - go and pack your things and he will be here at 2pm.

I was absolutely over the moon, ran back to the wing to tell the girls who were all shocked - I ironed my trousers, gave away my canteen and packed my bags.

Then Kemmie came and said there was a problem and I couldn't go till the morning - little disappointed but its only one night, then an hour later she came back and said she had made a terrible mistake and apologised, I wasn't going till next week - apparently she would not release me on license as I had not served a third of my sentence and she should have confirmed that before she told me - 'sorry' she said.

I was absolutely devastated, I told her that it's not the point that she's sorry she should never have given me that hope before confirmation that her information was correct. As desperate as I was, if I was at all suicidal as are many of the girls here, that would have tipped them over the edge. They cannot play with peoples emotions like this - I know I am not the first and if nothing is done, I won't be the last.

Mark came on his visit - I could see he was upset and had been crying, I just felt empty and I had no energy left to cry anymore. I am going to put in an official complaint as I hope Mark is - she cannot be allowed to continue to operate in this way or else they will have their first death in this prison - and it's only been open 8 weeks!

I've come back to my room, I am not unpacking my things, I will get out just what I need and that is it.

Then tonight we were all sitting at the table and Jenn was waiting by the phone, they called 5 minutes till lock up and then Jenn lost it, she flipped completely and pulled one of the girls out of the phone box and screamed at her - obviously all the guards came running and I went over to try and calm her down so that she didn't hit one of the officers. The girl was in a terrible state - god knows what's going to happen to Jenn, they could put her in the block for this or at the least behind doors - she does need some kind of anger management to control her temper, she just flies off the handle, one day it will get her into too much trouble, she has a good man and a chance for a good life, I really don't want to see her blow it.

Lock up time now and I can hear lots of movement in the wing but cannot see anything - I suppose in the morning we will know.'

Thursday 12th August 2004

'Today was okay - had my first art class in the morning, I am making my daughter a bracelet to send home, its only simple but I am sure she will love it. I don't think the boys would appreciate a bracelet though, I will have to think of something else for them, perhaps a bookmark!

The morning went quickly because I was doing something, but this afternoon dragged by - they moved another 5 people on to the wing - one with nits, another that looked like she had been dug up, and a nutter in a wheelchair that throws boiling water at everyone. I have never seen so many 'scagheads' in one place at one time. The one that looks like it has been dug up has been put next to me!

This afternoon there was talk that she had received a parcel - I thought they meant by post - oh no, apparently she had 'crutched' a parcel of crack, meaning she put drugs up her vagina - nice!

I was doing the washing up in the kitchen and one person came and got a pair of gloves and disappeared with them, didn't think much of it. Came out of the kitchen and it seems another six of the 'scags' had gone into her room and all got a piece of the drugs what a bunch of scum they all are. I am so glad I am moving soon, I can't stand all this

Doing time and serving your sentence is one thing but being faced with people cutting themselves, drug dealing, open lesbianism and filthy living habits and having to live with them is another - there is no excuse, I know I do not deserve this.

Rang home this afternoon - I knew my sister and Mum were there today - the kids were at Shawfire and Jacob and my sisters little girl were playing on playstation. I needed to speak to Mum because my daughter had said Nanny was getting annoyed because she hadn't heard from me and yet I had sent her two letters - I wanted to make sure she had got them - then when I spoke to her I realised my daughters letter was 2 weeks old!

I will ring home tomorrow night to speak to Mark and the kids.

Spoke to Melissa today - she hasn't had one visit in 8 weeks because all her family are in Ireland, and today they came to see her and they were told they only had one hour! Isn't that just outrageous. She was so upset, you would think they could allow a couple of hours under the circumstances, what with Melissa being 2052 (suicide watch). This prisons admin system is outrageous. Also, Barbara was meant to go to hospital today for some kind of special injection as she has cancer - she has been waiting for

2 weeks for it and the healthcare team here have been giving her paracetamol. When she got the hospital appointment for today she got up at 5.30am and waited for someone to take her - and waited, and waited. In the end she gave up and had another paracetamol - for cancer!

TJ was finally taken to hospital today, she has aids and they have only just discovered she has a huge blood clot in her leg so they rushed her to hospital.

Lisa has been told her baby is not growing and needs a regular scan to monitor the babys weight - she went for one scan and has heard no more, she is worried sick. I can see we are going to have to deliver this baby on the dining table here on 2B!

Oh well, another day over, another day nearer, by the time I move next Tuesday I will have done 4 weeks - almost half my sentence.'

Friday 13th August 2004

'Had the art class again this morning and made another bracelet - a daisy chain one, really enjoyed it, I will definitely start doing it at home I think, very therapeutic.

Came back for lunch, couldn't sit at the table because of all the scum that has moved in so I had lunch in my room and fell asleep. I woke to the sound of them locking me in, they didn't let us out till 6pm for dinner hardly ate anything.

Went for a lap around the yard and then back in to be locked up for the night. I didn't mind really because it's the opening ceremony of the Olympics tonight so that's nice to watch. Rang home and spoke to Mark and the children, bless them all.

Wrote to Sarah, got a letter from Mum, my sister and my brother's wife - hopefully once I move perhaps I will be able to have more visits and then my sister, Mum and friend will be able to come and see me.

Found out today that what I was talking about yesterday wasn't as simple as I thought - apparently the one that looks like she's been dug up did 'crutch' a parcel and someone found out about it but she didn't offer it round so the six that I saw going into her room with a pair of gloves took the drugs from her crutch - by force! Another girl that was in there wanted to go out when she realised what was going on, they slapped her and made her stay and slapped the other girl and forced her and took the drugs out from her and they all then shared the drugs leaving the girl in tears - apparently they call it 'de-crutching' here and apparently its quite common!

Get me out of here for fucks sake! Now its just me, Lisa, Jenn, Trish, Vicki and Keely that keep together and don't trust anyone.'

Saturday 14th August 2004

'News today is that the individuals concerned are

going to be charged with rape and buggery. We are all being locked up because of what's gone on and there has to be an officer on duty at all times. The girl has gone to hospital with internal damage and the people being charged are locked in their cells.

Done wing cleaning today because nobody else bothered – they're all sitting around stoned staring into space - Jesus, anyone that's thinking of doing drugs ought to spend one week in prison to see what it does to people - that will put them off!!

Got letters this morning from Mum, my sister and brothers wife. My sister's letter had to be 8 pages long just so that she could beat my cousin- typical, she's always got to be one better! Nothing changes there then eh!

Well now its 8.20pm, we're all locked up, another day over. Went to the gym this afternoon - because I've cut down on the potatoes I've gone back down to 10stone - thank goodness. I refuse to go home heavier that when I came in and I am determined to grow my hair again.

They've now moved the people to the block and officially charged them - the whole prison is talking about it, we've had another load of girls move in - wonder what the night will bring!

Goodnight my honies, sleep tight!'

Sunday 15th August 2004

'Went to church this morning and had a sing along as usual, then come back for lunch, fell asleep after lunch for an hour then went outside and sat with the girls.

The 'yardies' (jamaican girls) started doing relay races, then the other girls joined in, then the guards joined in - it was really good fun and made the afternoon go quickly, two of the guards (Damian & Karl) were really fast and beat the girls - shame on us!! Good giggle, much better than fighting, there's actually a nice atmosphere when everyone's joining in having fun - makes the day go quicker too.

While we were outside somebody called 'Mel' came up to me and said she knew all about me etc, she started to explain that her friend works with Michelle – Marks work partner's girlfriend (and Marks previous girlfriend actually) and that she knew all about what I'd done etc - I was pretty annoyed I can tell you - not that I'm ashamed of it, but I don't like strangers coming up to me to try and be your friend in here. I like to keep myself to myself, that way nobody knows what your'e gonna do, so they leave you alone.

I've made plenty of new acquaintances in here - but I most certainly do not want one of Michelle's friends to try to be my friend! In here you have no friends, only acquaintances!

I hope I'm still on line to move on Tuesday.'

Monday 16th August 2004

'Went to Art class this morning and managed to finish my bracelets and necklaces and I got permission to take them with me. I checked that I'm still due to go tomorrow – god knows what time though! Hopefully it will be early to get myself settled, I know I will be upset but I have to look forward and think positive.

This afternoon went slow and I nearly laid on my bed and fell asleep.

Put my washing in to be done and I lose one pair of pyjamas, 2 pairs of knickers and had to search for my trousers and tops, 3 different people had them in with their clothes. Still got no p.j.'s so it looks like I've lost them – great eh.

No visit today so I expect they wouldn't let Mark in – never mind, I will see him at the new place. Finished pills today and I haven't got a doctor's appointment despite putting in a request two weeks ago! Hopefully at the new place they will be organized and I can get another appointment.'

Tuesday 17th August

'Went to the art class this morning but they came and pulled me out – time to move, I was so excited, it was so nice to see the outside world, to see conkers on the trees, cars on the road, people shopping – funny how you take things for granted.

We dropped three other people off at Cookham Wood and then we went on to East Sutton Park – beautiful surroundings. We passed lovely villages and lovely houses – then we got here, it looks like a castle, really old, beautiful gardens etc but Jesus is it in need of an overhaul! Trust me to think of the condition of the building! They showed me to the dormitory and I wanted to cry – no privacy at all and there are 10 women to the dorm, absolutely bloody awful, I just want my cell back so I can cry on my own.'

It's now 9.40 and I have come down to the drawing room (the 'quiet room'), a nice area with chesterfields and armchairs around and a big old fireplace and all the daily newspapers on the table, a little bit of peace and sanity – the only bit of peace and sanity! The girls in the dorm just had a row about me and a girl called Karina talking over the TV and they were trying to watch something – I do not feel very welcome at all – in fact it is horrid.

I'm sure tomorrow I will feel different – I can remember crying when I moved to block 2 from block 3 but now it all feels like it was home and I do wish I was back there again.

I just hope I get a job Friday and the time will be go quicker then – tomorrow I am just going to take Harry Potter into the garden and sit and read to escape my mind – its only 6 weeks to go, I have to remember that.

Bad night tonight – I feel like crying but there is nowhere to cry – feeling very depressed and just want this nightmare to be over.

It seems like there are a lot of girls here who are doing long sentences – I would not do a long sentence, I could not do a long sentence, I would have to end it, the thought of only 6 weeks is all that keeps me going.

Wednesday 18th August 2004

'Well today was not much better – I really wish I had never moved – the girls here are okay – better than Bronzefield but there just isn't that friendly, jokey feeling – the staff are much more severe and definitely no first name terms here! I miss the staff as much as I do the inmates and my single cell. I hate sharing a dorm, I am just such a private person.

I helped out at the stores today so that made the day go quite quickly – packing together all the canteen orders.

The Governor called me down to his office today to tell me to tell my sister to stop ringing him. She is becoming a bit of a pain asking for extra visits so that Mum and she can come along to visit as well as Mark and the kids. She obviously doesn't understand this system, if I get preferential treatment for whatever reason, the girls will look at me as if I'm Miss Goody Two Shoes and that leads to trouble, which I certainly do not want, not again, so then I had to ring my sister and say that she and Mum could come along on the second half of the visit.

Then they let me ring Mark with an officer present and I told him, he wasn't very happy about sharing a visit but they will all have to compromise – as I have to here!

I tried to ring Mark on my phonecard but the number wasn't put on yet so I couldn't call but then I was called again to the centre office, Mark had rung, worried because I hadn't rung him, so again I couldn't really talk to him properly but he asked if I was okay – he can tell by my voice how I feel, I got really upset again. Hopefully my phone will be on tomorrow so I can talk to him properly in private.'

Thursday 19th August 2004

'Actually slept last night okay for the first time.

Called up by the centre office today – they had read my letter that I sent out to home last night and thought that I had used 'inappropriate language' where I had referred to escaping as a joke – they were really snotty about it, probably because I said it was crap here and the staff were shit! Looks like I'll be picked on by the staff now – what a fuck up.

Had induction this morning and then this afternoon I helped out in stores again – it was okay and the day has gone quite fast thankfully, much better than yesterday.

Rang home tonight, nobody there so I rang my sister, only to be greeted by a snotty unwelcome – when I asked what was wrong, she replied 'your bloke – that's what's wrong, you need to talk to him, he's being abusive to me and mum and we can't take it no more'.

I told her I had had a shitty day yesterday, to which she replied 'so have I', then told me if I wanted a conversation to ring Mum instead, said 'bye' and that was it, phone dead. I wished I hadn't wasted my phone credit on her now. So selfish, what keeps me going in here is knowing that it's all okay at home – I can't be worrying about doing this and home, but she just doesn't understand. She sees everything through her eyes, sees things for what they look like not what they are.

She had a shitty day – she wants to attempt to spend one night in here!'

Friday 20th August 2004

'Had education interview today – he said I was too intelligent to do any of the courses and I wasn't here long enough to do an NVQ – choices pretty limited then!!

I put in a governor's appointment to start a crafts class so that at least we could make things to send home, at least that would give me something interesting to do.

The labour board sat today and although I said 'farm, farm, farm', I got kitchens, I told them as soon as I start, I will be putting in a request to change. I was really looking forward to working on the farm – so disappointed. Wrote to Mum in the morning and then wrote to my sister in the afternoon. I spent the evening doing little drawings to send to the children and then I had to do one of Shrek's face for my big hero from his little princess!

Wrote to Debbie today too – Mark had sent me lots of cards and letters from home which was lovely – in amongst them there was a letter from Debbie saying she was due to come here in the next 2 weeks but the letter was dated 10th so she could be here this week! Anyway, I warned her that at first it is a real big shock and it takes some real adjusting to the dorms – I still hate the dorms but I am adjusting.

Karinna and I spent the night laying on our beds chatting – she was telling me about her life and how this has made her see that celebrities, money and fame mean nothing.

She was due to do an article in FHM before she came here, the newspapers are trying to find her as she slept with a very famous England football player who's married called J… T…. (I know nothing about football so his name meant nothing to me), at the moment on Sky they are showing a documentary on lap dancers that she filmed a year ago! She is really worried that it is all going to come out at the same time and she will be moved from here to closed prison because it is too easy for the press to get to her here.

It was amazing to hear how much money she makes in one day and then how much she spends on clothes, shoes, handbags etc – and she's only 24!

She has a nice family behind her and some real good friends – I am positive her life will be different when she gets out – just after me. She does see things the same as me – life is too precious to waste on being bitter or angry with anyone – in here teaches you that much for sure.'

Sunday 24th August 2004

'Today has gone really slow for some reason. We all have to do a housekeeping job in the morning which takes all of 10 minutes then I spent the rest of the morning in the drawing room reading the newspaper. Had lunch and then in the afternoon went into the garden to do some sketching, it was quite nice actually, I sat in the garden by the big conker tree just in front of the church and done a sketch of the old church – such a pretty church, it's a shame it's not used too much. Well, while I was drawing one of the

girls came and sat over with me, Linda, I knew she was having a visit but apparently her husband didn't turn up – well she was really fed up obviously, but I sat and chatted to her and then she said she was going to get changed so I carried on. Well, that night at dinner they called out her name for roll-call but no answer. They searched the house and grounds – gone!

I felt really strange, I was more worried that she had done something silly but the girls said that she wasn't like that – so she must have done a runner! I can't make it out, she only had till November.

Spent the night chatting with Karinna, was meant to go on playstation but a film 'The Score' came on so we watched that in bed.'

Sunday 22nd August 2004

'Scary day today, the kids are coming to visit for the first time – my whole morning was focused around the visit, I had a shower, washed my hair, then straightened it, then sat in the drawing room reading newspapers until my name was called. I wanted to run to the visit centre but I kept control – as soon as I saw them, Jacob ran straight over into my arms, then my daughter Rachel and my son Thomas, then Mark hugged all of us – big group hug, then Jacob said 'someone's squeezing me' It did make me laugh. We all had a little cry but then it was okay – I was amazed, Jacob gave me loads of cuddles, he was fine,

Rachel was listening to my every word and Thomas was busy drinking all the coke and sweets he could.

The visit went fine – I think if anything the kids got bored – I could sense that Mark wanted to say loads but couldn't because the kids were there. Thomas's voice seems so deep and Jacob has really shot up in height – Rachel didn't seem to have changed much bless her, Jacob gave me a big cuddle sitting on my lap and said 'when will you be coming home with us Mummy?', I said well next week, you can come and see me again, then the week after and then the week after I can come home.

I thought by that time he would have lost count of weeks so it probably will be time for me to come home. Rachel said she rang my sister to ask if she could pick her up from Shawfire's but she said 'no' which has really pissed me off – whatever her problem with Mark is, she does not make my children suffer and Mum has announced she's going on holiday for a week with my sister! It's great when families stick together eh! What's that saying 'blood is thicker than water', almost laughable… its the summer holidays and my kids are stuck at home in this situation, the least they could do was take them away for a week if they were going away, but that's selfish of me to think like that and want the best for my children I guess?

The kids told me that the fox got into the chicken run and got Rolo but Rocky fought him off and gave himself a stroke. Margaret took him to the vet and he died – I was really upset – my poor brave Rocky – I loved him from when he was an egg. Thomas said they have buried him in the garden and we will go and get another cockerel when I come home. I know he was old anyway, but he had been so brave and I wasn't there… Isn't it silly what things really upset you when you least expect it.'

Monday 23rd August 2004

'First day of work today – yuk!

Really didn't like it - just can't stand cleaning/kitchen work, made worse by the fact that there is hardly anything to do and you end up just standing around waiting for them to stop cooking so you can start cleaning.

One bit of good news is that Sabrina wants to come off the farm and go into the kitchens so I will see Mr Chan tomorrow and ask him to swap.

The day went quite fast today – wrote to mum with a little card telling her she can have the first hour on Sunday.

Picked my property up today that Mark brought in for me – lovely pillowcase, he got pictures of me and the children printed all over it for me so that I can sleep next to them – bless. Oh yes, and a t-shirt with 'there goes Mr & Mrs Jones' but I don't think I will be wearing that in here, I think he's getting quite excited about the idea of us being married – nearly as much as me.

Had a long chat with Herbie today as the situation re Mark/my sister was really playing on my mind. I know the children are fine but that's not enough, I want my whole family to be okay. She pretty much reflected what I already knew, when you're in a place like this you cannot allow yourself to worry about others and what they might think – it takes all your mental energy to concentrate on keeping your mind through this. She spoke a lot of sense. She said at the end of the day they are all adults and they will all have to compromise and find their own way through this situation just as I have to, without causing any more heartbreak and suffering.

It's so sad, I was so happy to hear they were all like one big family – it all made it so much easier, but now, nobody can understand except the other girls in here, how it feels to know there is turmoil at home – I find myself sitting staring out of the window thinking about nothing in particular and then my mind drifts into how they must all feel – Mark pissed off that my sister has tried to 'take over' his family, my sister rejected because Mark doesn't want her over there, and Mum probably caught in the middle not knowing where to turn and nobody to talk to about it. It just annoys me, I can see Marks point because I know how controlling my sister can be and she does not take constructive criticism at all, why couldn't she just show understanding and back off a little without getting the major hump, and blowing everything out of proportion – at such a crucial time. I realise that Mark and my sister are both stubborn and controlling and the pair of them are as bad as each other, but its not about them, its about the children and for once I was asking them both to put aside their feelings and suck it up no matter how much it goes against how they feel, but knowing the pair of them and how stubborn they are, they won't. They would both suffer in silence than apologise and make things better – just for the time I am here I cannot do anything to avoid this situation, its all out of my hands…

I just know what Dad would say – he would tell my sister not to interfere, Dad would help Mark with the children because he knows what it's like to be alone with a small child – regardless of any situation, but Dad was never selfish.

In Marks letter to me today, he said he thought about my Dad and was amazed at the strength he must have had to have brought me up the way he has on his own, pushing to the side his own feelings and doing things to ensure that I was okay – I think it actually sunk in with Mark, the kind of man my Dad was – I wish he had known him like I did, or do still. But there again, it sounds like he did know him well!

Weird eh, Dad was abandoned to bring me up, now Mark has been abandoned to bring up my children, only difference here is it is not my choice and I will be going back as soon as I can and will be back forever – no matter what.'

Wednesday 25th August 2004

'Well the good news is that I didn't get time to write in yesterday's diary – that's a first!

The other good news is I have found someone on the farm that wants to work in the kitchen – so I am going to try and do a job swap with them so I have been running around all day getting my form signed and approved by everyone so that its ready for the labour board on Friday – hopefully if its approved, I could start on Monday, what a difference that would make for me.

Felt really tired today – these mornings having to be up and doing toast for 100 people by 7am is taking its toll – I could have easily fallen back to sleep this afternoon, I am conscious that I haven't had time to go to the gym at all or do any exercise – must start doing something, even if it is just jogging round the garden.

Got another letter from Debbie-Anne today – she's been told the first week in September she will be coming here – wrote back to her today.'

Thursday 26th August 2004

'Can't believe it's nearly the weekend again – it seems to have really come round quickly.

Really tired today, getting up at 7am to do breakfast is getting to me, I really hope the Labour Board goes my way tomorrow, I know that the interest of being on the farm will make the time go quicker for me too.

Got a letter from Mark today – bless him and I also got a postcard from Greg (brother), would you believe it, 5 years not a word and then, out of the blue a postcard calling me 'poppet' and signing off 'love as always' – I wonder if he sent it to the wrong person – strange lot my family eh!

I am going to keep to my word, as hard as it may be, you only have one life and so easily it can be taken away from you – there is no point holding grudges, if only everyone could see it that way eh! I think this thing with my sister and Mum will take more than willpower – I hope not because I just want to have a happy family, I don't want any animosity between anyone, but things don't always work that way, do they!'

Friday 27th August 2004

'Well, the good news today is that I have been given a job on the farm starting Monday – yippee, now I can see the time left is going to go so much quicker. I was

dreading having to go into the kitchens next week, but now I'm looking forward to Monday.

Got a letter today from Jo – she said she rang Mark but he was so upset she didn't like to ask him so I sat down tonight and started to write to Jo, I've stopped for a break now at page 5 but I will go back to it tomorrow!

Still no word from Mum or my sister, I tried to ring Mum yesterday but she is still on answerphone, so I still don't know what is going on the weekend, I shall be so angry if they don't turn up because I would have wasted half a visit – but on the other hand I don't know what to say to them – I know that whatever I say I will show my disappointment.

Chatting to Karina tonight, she has helped me so much through this 'change' to here, we do seem to be on the same wavelength and I find it helpful to air my views to her, just as (hopefully) she does to me.

I was chatting as well, to one of the girls here – 'T', shes a real nice girl, bit of a tomboy, from New Zealand, well, I was chatting to her and she was saying about her resettlement plan and how she was coming out next year, so I asked her how long she had been in for – 11 years!!! God, was I shocked – I knew for that kind of sentence it had to be bad –made a few enquiries and was told she had come here as a 'hitman' to specifically kill people in cold blood – I could not believe it, obviously she was now a reformed character, but the shock that she had killed someone!

I must admit that I have learned here not to ask people about their crime and how long because the majority of people here are lifers for one reason or another and mostly have long sentences. There is a girl in our room who is a lifer for killing her stepchild – gossip is that she molested her children but I won't ask her the details. Another girl in here was trafficking drugs and got 12 years – imagine that, well I just can't.

Some of the people here seem so nice and helpful – there is never any rows – a few bitchy comments but that is it, they seem too nice to have done something so bad – but as I say, I have learned not to judge, but more not to ask because in the majority you don't like the answer.

Even the guard said most people here have done long sentences and are at the end of their time and need to be resettled into the community. It still shocks me though to learn that someone you have come to care for and respect could have murdered a person (or more than one in a lot of cases).'

Saturday 28th August 2004

'Tried to ring Mum again today but still on answerphone – I've heard nothing from either Mum or my sister since I have been here – nearly 2 weeks –

I left a message saying I won't keep trying to ring anymore, I've had enough, god knows what is going to happen Sunday – what the hell are we going to talk about – if they turn up that is! Oh fuck it, I'm not going to waste any more emotion on thinking about what they are doing.

Got a letter today from Jo so I sat and done a letter to her this afternoon, 12 pages later – poor girl, she will regret asking me how I feel.

Last day working in the kitchen today – thank goodness, I'm actually looking forward to Monday now.

We had bingo tonight in the drawing room, started off quite a giggle, Mr Reed was calling the balls and No. 69 came out, one of the girls called out because she missed the number before it – "what comes before 69" she asked. Mr Reed replied "foreplay usually". Which got quite a laugh, but then the bingo went on for over 2 hours and I had definitely lost the will to live by then – my eyes were closing on their own accord.'

Sunday 29th August 2004

'Good day today – had Carnival Queen competition this evening – was really good fun – helped to make the costumes and all the girls were dancing that 'Shake your booty' style, one dance that I freely admit I cannot do – I think my age is against me on that

one, but it's fun to watch and some of those girls are the best dancers you will ever see, really good evening and lifted everyone's spirits – but sad to think all these sad girls were so happy, if only for one night.

Dreading the visit today and what I was going to say to Mum and my sister, considering I haven't heard from them for 10 days! My mind is so confused. They started trying to say what had happened, I knew they were going to blame Mark for it all and I know better than that so I just told them to stop – I wasn't interested in what happened, I can't deal with it here so I shall deal with it on the out – then they moved onto other things. I was amazed, I didn't cry once and I didn't hold their hands, I didn't feel close to them at all.

After the hour, Mark and the children came in, Mum and my sister said goodbye to me and the kids and off they went. After 10 minutes Mark calmed down, at first he was just shaking with anger and didn't say anything – if I'm honest it upset me that he allowed his feelings for them to ruin our time but luckily he soon snapped out of it and we had a good visit – the kids were much better than last week and we all took our chairs into the garden and I could play with them which was lovely.

After the visit I was sitting on my bed and I had to write to them all telling them what I felt – because they all completely ignored everyone, it brought back that terrible feeling of unease that there used to be at home and I didn't like it, in fact it made me dread going home, and I will not have that feeling after being through this shit. I have told them all that whatever they need to do, get on and do it, but I will not have them ignoring each other - any of them or else I will not be in their company. I have wanted to be home so much for so long, I will not allow their bitterness, anger, stubbornness – whatever it is to make me feel that I don't want to be there, I don't have a choice! if I am going to be confronted by all three of them, in that situation – if they get the hump with what I have said – tough! I have changed and I will not tolerate it – my life and the life of my children is too precious to waste on bad feelings.'

Monday 30th August 2004

'Had a good day today, it was Sports Day here at ESP, I was just going along to watch but in the end me and Kaz won the 3 legged race and won a chocolate bar so then we had a go at welly throwing and won another chocolate bar, then the dressing up game and got another chocolate bar. At the end of the day I had a good stash to take back to my room! Then after that, we had a BBQ which was really nice and we all stuffed our faces.

I rang home tonight, I knew the kids were over my sisters today and when I rang, I felt so guilty at sending them letters, I spoke to Mark and he sounded so sad – he was on a bad day and missing me badly and I had just sent him a letter telling him what I thought – he so desperately wanted to know how much I loved him. So I then wrote another letter saying sorry for the first one and told him how much I loved him, missed him, cant wait to be with him again, hopefully that will cheer him up again – I do realise how hard it must be for him out there, all alone and having to cope with everything, I just wish I could do something!'

Tuesday 31st August 2004

'Had a letter from Sally and Andy today, really nice card letting me know they are thinking of me and telling me to be strong and not to give up – really wanted to cry – it felt so nice to think that the others are thinking of me in a kind way and not what I was expecting at all – I will write to her to thank her.

Mark and the children sent me a letter today and a lovely picture from Jacob – they are all looking forward to Sunday – tomorrow is the first day of September, we're getting there.

Had a good day at work – very busy from 8.30 till 4pm moving pigs from one field to another, moving cows, horses and sheep. Some of the pigs and cows are a bit scary because the boars have big teeth and they try and corner you in the pen to have a sniff to see who you are – the cows (bulls) just look at you as if to say 'you dare touch my bottom with that prong and I will charge at you!'. But the good side is that the piglets are just so cute – we had to move one loft of 13 with their mum into a new pen today – mum came in all right but we had to put the litter into a wheelbarrow to move them, oh it was so funny, what a picture all you could see was all their little heads poking out of the top of the wheelbarrow – if only I could have taken a picture…'

Wednesday 1st September 2004

'Oh for so long, I have been waiting for this day – 27 days to go. Funny how things turn out. Mark had the right hump with me sending that letter – our conversation tonight must have lasted all of 3 minutes – he said he felt like he was being told off like a kid, after all he had done and 6 weeks of hell at home – he'd had enough. Basically I cut the conversation short – there was nothing I could say to him to make it any better – I had told him how I felt and he didn't like it. I said I would ring tomorrow but I have just written him another letter telling him it wasn't my intention to hurt him, I just had to get it off my chest. My head is so confused what am I supposed to do – I know Mum and my sister done wrong but I know the way he talks to people with no respect whatsoever – so in my eyes they are all to blame, and I told them. I suppose at the end of the day its none of them to blame, its all my fucking fault for being here.

I know what Mark feels like at the moment but at least he has the constant reminder of why he's doing it – here I have no reminders and could easily be on self-destruct and press the ultimate 'fuck it all' button – BOLLOCKS TO THE FUCKING WORLD

Enough of that, I had a good day on the farm – we were stacking hay/straw this morning off the trailer onto the haybale, pretty scary up there y'know – my foot kept falling between the bales and disappearing – had a tractor ride back with Mr B which was fun.

Then I had to muck out the pigs and as I lifted the hay/poo, there was a big lump in it – a dead piglet, I started jumping up and down shouting 'dead pig, dead pig' hysterically shaking my head and hands, 'oops sorry' said Mr B 'forgot to tell you about that' then started laughing as if he had planned that, I think that was my initiation into the farm that day – rotten lot…

Two of the pigs had their litters yesterday – 8 piglets each, cutest things. Came back absolutely shattered, I think I could go to sleep at 8pm tonight and actually sleep for probably the first time ever.

Such a shame, I had so much to say today for a change and Mark didn't want to talk to me, hopefully by Sunday he will be okay and love me again – if not, we've got a whole 2 hours of non-talking!

Jacob starts school tomorrow so it will be a lot easier all round and the kids go back Friday, strange to think I won't be there on his first day of school…

Things at ESP are getting better – even getting friendlier with the girls in the dorm – plaited Karinna's hair last night – it was wild me, Kaz, Marlene and Karina were all watching Twister yesterday, it was almost like a girls pyjama party, we were all sharing our sweets round, it was nice.

I am supposed to go to Education tomorrow but I don't particularly want to – I would much rather be on the farm.'

Thursday 2nd September 2004

'Its 6.45pm and I am sitting out in the garden watching the world go by, it's been a funny old day.

I can't stop thinking about how Mark must be feeling, thinking that I don't care about him and don't appreciate what he is going through too, but I do. I love him dearly but a phone call or letter to reinforce that is not enough but it is all that I have at the moment.

When I am working, it takes my mind off of things at home, why I am here, where I am, the kids, everything, I just concentrate on the animals and it all seems okay, they need me to look after them and I guess that kind of makes up for me not being able to look after my own children, who knows.

Today we had to cut the piglets teeth and give them their iron injection, they were all snuggling up to me because they were scared and I was nice and warm, it was a lovely feeling, safe and secure, they are just so cute.

Then we had to go down and clear some bramble bushes and cut down some trees. While we were there we picked some blackberries to eat for our tea break, we had to balance on the most awkward branches so that we could pick the biggest juiciest ones and then put them in a pile on our gloves, but while we were busy cutting fences, the cows came along and eat the bloody lot!

God did I ache today from all that straw carting yesterday – I had to roll out of bed today but I soon forgot about it once I was working – no doubt I will ache again later.

It's now 6.55pm and there are 3 hot air balloons floating across the horizon from the dorm window – how nice it must be for them people up there – I wonder where they are going and if they have any idea we are watching them locked up in here.

Two new people came today from Cookham Wood, but not Debbie she wrote to me and said they have promised her a place at the end of September – probably my place, typical eh.

Wrote to the kids and Mark, Sally and Andy and my brothers wife today, I'm going in now to try to ring home.'

Friday 3rd September 2004

'Felt better this morning , got Marks letter (13 pages) and he did get it off his chest but not in a nasty way – I was very proud of him. Apparently she has told him that he take his kid and she will have mine! I did question whether she did say that but the scary thing is I can imagine her saying that, if anything ever did happen to me in here, there's no way them children are to be split up, no matter what, that's the sort of comment she would say, well it doesn't work with my family! Wrote to home to tell them all I love them. I am fighting battles between my family from in here and it just doesn't work, I haven't got the mental strength to cope with it all so I've just got to let them get on with it, its just beyond words.

Had a good day at work, feeding pigs, checking the stock, which involves walking across all the fields counting sheep, horses, cows and making sure they are all okay – nice time, time for me to think about things and empty my head – I'm going to miss the farm when I go, whoever thought I would say that?'

Sunday 5th September 2004

'I had the longest lay-in I have had in prison history

(well, mine at least!), I didn't even wake up until 8.25am!! Went down for breakfast, went and read the paper, had a shower, dried and straightened my hair – then it was time for a visit. Jacob ran straight over to me and jumped into my arms which was lovely – we all had a nice visit, Rachel looked like she was in desperate need of Mums cuddles, luckily we were allowed outside so we parked ourselves up under the tree and all lay there cuddling, one on top of the other, the only one who didn't climb on board was Thomas – I am so desperate to be at home with them children I cannot tell you, I so just want to hug them and watch them fall asleep, cut their hair, plait my daughters hair, everything really that I usually do. I don't know how people cope with long sentences and I thank god that I am nearly out, any longer and I think the children would be damaged beyond repair – I can see sadness in their eyes that they are not letting out – much longer and that sadness will turn to anger and bitterness. Tonight I will pray for my tag date to come through, so that I have a definite date and something to aim for.'

Monday 6th September 2004

'Oh, I give up, I've booked my mum and sister in for visit on Sunday because Mark and the kids are coming down for Childrens Day on the Saturday, then when I rang Mark tonight, he said 'good news,

I've just found out that we can visit on Sunday too' when I told him that mum and sister were coming down, he went all quiet and stroppy – I can't bloody well win I tell you. I rang mum early on in the day, she was upset, by all the bad feelings at home, I asked her to pop round home a couple of days per week between 4pm and 6pm so that the kids can at least keep contact – its only a few more weeks now – I'm not going to try and tear myself between all of them anymore – things will be my way or no way. I'm sick of trying to please them all – so I will please me now.

Not had a very good day today – I had the day off and was going to take my book, CD player into the garden and get some colour on my legs but it was really overcast so I haven't been out at all. Feeling a bit depressed by the whole situation today and I really just want to be at home so I can cuddle the kids and try to make good all the bad feelings at home.'

Tuesday 7th September 2004

'Better day today back at work, had a chat with Mrs C and she said when I have a bad day like yesterday I can always go over the farm!

I would even work on the farm longer than my sentence as long as I can go home at night!

Had a letter from Sally again today – really nice, she sent me a little poem that just summed it all up perfectly, titled Hang in There

Sometimes there are bad days
When life becomes a fight
And all that you can do
Is to hang on in there tight,

Remember dawn comes after darkness
And the fiercest storms don't last
In the future this hard present
Will become a distant past,

So here's a simple message
I hope that you will heed it
I'm always here to help you
So call me if you need it.

I am going to put this on the computer and give a copy to all those here that I have made friends with because I know it will help them too.

We were mucking out the pigs today when Sandra went over to the house to hang the curtains ready for the new garden person to move into on Monday. She came out and burst into tears – it took 10 minutes to console her and ask her what was the matter – it turned out it was the first house she had seen the inside of in 12 years – with that, we all burst into tears, we all knew what she meant, one of the simplest things in life that you just take for granted – having a home.

Wrote back to Sally and also wrote to Bridget (Frazier's mum) as she wrote to me too – it's weird to think that I never really knew her on the outside but she felt that she needed to write to me to let me know how she felt and to put my mind at ease – how nice is that, it kind of renews your faith in human nature and the world is still a beautiful place – in spite of all its downfalls.'

Wednesday 8th September 2004

'I am actually writing this on Thursday as I forgot to write in here yesterday. Had probation at 9.00am which was quite interesting – she said she sent my papers off on Monday for my probation – by law they have 10 days to reply which gives them till next Friday at the latest and if the prison hasn't heard anything they get on their case then, the probation lady (Amanda) said she can't see any reason at all why it would be delayed – when it comes back she has to do a report and then the Governor has to approve it and that's it – off you go! Sounded quite promising and gave me some hope. I rang Mark as soon as I knew and left a message on his mobile. The phone still isn't working at home – I just hope its mended before the probation people come round home.

I had quite a compliment today at work – Mrs C at the farm said it was a shame that I wasn't staying longer, she enjoys working with me, it's nice to have somebody 'normal' there, what a compliment, but I did have to inform her that I had no intention of prolonging my stay – not even for the pigs!'

Thursday 9th September 2004

'Had I.T. this morning and wrote a copy of the poem that Sally sent me out for the girls on the computer and laminated them. The education Manager liked the poem so much that he put a copy on the wall of the Education Department to give hope to everyone (so I made sure I put my name on the bottom).

My last class of I.T. today, I took myself off the register, I would rather spend the time on the farm than there doing something I already know.

Lorraine (A) has been funny with me today – I must have upset her about something but I don't know what – wish she would just tell me what's annoyed her rather than ignoring me and acting bitchy and childlike – makes it very difficult to share a room with her – but there again, I haven't got long, just leave her to get on with it! I've nearly run out of pages, I think I should just finish this book by the time I leave.

Had a good chat with April today, I feel for her, she obviously cannot move on and is very guarded, she may be loud and showy, but it's just a front really – she is shy and insecure.

They told us today that they had made a mistake with the visits on Sunday, we are not allowed a visit on Sunday and the Childrens Day, so I had to ring mum and let her know that the visit is off – she wasn't in but I left a message on her answerphone – I will ring her tomorrow, hopefully she will be okay about it, if not, there's not a lot I can do about it. The weather for the weekend looks like it's going to be awful – typical eh.'

Friday 10th September 2004

'Spoke to mum today – she's done to her neck what Jacob done to his ages ago, she's in agony. I did feel for her so I said I would ring her over the weekend to see how she is –she said that my sister was ringing her everyday, so as long as someone is taking care of her then that's okay.

She was okay about Sundays visit, she said that Sean (brother) was coming but my sister couldn't for whatever reason. Personally I think she is struggling with it all judging by the card she sent me and lack of conversation or love contained within – but I cant do nothing from here – I wont ring her again because of last time but I sent her a letter today.

Spoke to Mark today – I think he's looking forward to tomorrow too – I told him that I've put his mum and nephew on the list too.

Telephone still not working at home but apparently BT were there and it should be working by tomorrow.'

Saturday 11th September

'Childrens Day today – went really well, Marks mum and nephew came too, the kids had a good time, we said they could stay as long as they wanted and they stayed from 11am to 3pm and then Marks Mum took them back to her place and gave me and Mark a bit of time to ourselves.

The kids all seemed fine, Rachel had a bit of trouble from Nancy at school (a so called friend) apparently she got the hump with Rachel over something and told everyone at school that I was in prison – luckily all Rachel's friends are supportive to her so she was okay – but how spiteful kids are!

Mark was okay – desperate for us to be together – we soon will be, it wont be long now. He's taking them to Tunbridge Wells tomorrow to buy some clothes for them all.

The kids have got a family party next Saturday and probably sleepover – if it wasn't for the party, I don't think Thomas would want to go, Pete hasn't seen the kids for 3 weeks and he had a go at him for wearing old trainers, what a joke, he knows I'm in here, he hasn't offered once to take them for a couple of days or offered any extra money or help to Mark for them – I hope them children see the light soon as to what he is really like when it comes to the crunch, so selfish but always has been, I shouldn't expect any more.'

Sunday 12th September 2004

'Up at 5.30am today – good god was it cold, soon got warm though mucking out the pigs etc – finished by 8.30am and in for breakfast.

Didn't do much all day – some girls had visits but I just lay on my bed reading my new book, got really engrossed in it, thank goodness for Susan Howatch!

Back to work for 3pm till 4.30pm chasing pigs, checking horses – actually went in the front of the Land Rover this morning – which felt weird, something you don't think about, but in a place like this you don't get to sit in a normal seat of a car much! I think I've actually discovered that although there are lots of things to get used to that feel weird, it wont actually take long to get used to normal things again.

Felt very tired today, there was a step class on but I couldn't even be bothered to go to that either so I went to bed early and slept really well, even though the telly and lights were on in the dorm till 11.00pm.'

Monday 13th September 2004

'What a day! Woke up at 7am and looked round, it was dark, miserable and everyone was still in bed so I

went back to sleep thinking it was 6am but oh no, it was time to get up, it was cold, wet, damp and raining and dark – I'm glad it's my day off, I think I will lay in bed all day, watch TV and read my book.

Heard from Tee that one of the mummy pigs died last night leaving 8 piglets – looks like we will have to feed them all by hand now – poor little things.

Spoke to Mark tonight, phones back on at home thank god, but they wouldn't divert it because it's not in his name so I tried to ring BT from here but no good – told Mark to ring probation tomorrow to tell them his mobile number to ring to organize the visit to home.'

Tuesday 14th September 2004

'Back to work today, the piglets have all survived so far and they look fighting fit so it looks good – there was chaos today – the lambs got in with the sheep, the pigs got out and only 3 of us turned up!

Rang Mark tonight to find out about probation – he rang and said they had a conversation with Mark – done the report there and then and are sending it back now! Yippee – it looks like it should all be on schedule for 29th – you wouldn't believe how relieved I feel.

Lots of letters in the post today – one card from Greg in Canada, Mark sent me the letter from my old work which I will have to reply to and about 4 letters from home, along with drawings and flowers – lovely aaaaarrrrgghhhh. (they are now stuck on my wall next to my bed).'

Thursday 16th September 2004

'Can't believe I missed a day – this week is going so quick, I can't believe it's nearly over, still haven't actually heard a date but hopefully the probation papers would have come through this morning.

Last night I got called to centre office and they done my risk assessment so next weekend I should be able to go out on town visits which will be nice, not to go home though, but to have a day out down Hastings or something.

Got a letter from mum today, not really saying much, got another card from Greg yesterday from Canada, got letters from Mark and the children and some pictures that he took on the childrens day – really lovely.

Busy day at work today there was only me and Sandra in, had a good conversation with Sandra about how she felt etc, she told me that she asked to be hung for her crime because she wanted to kill herself but didn't want to take the blame for taking her own life because she had a daughter – that daughter is now 27 and she's glad she didn't die – she's looking to be released in 3 years, after having served 12 years, she said she owes her life to her daughter – it was her husband she murdered, yet she admitted she loved him every day of his life and yet I would trust her with my life.

April, on the other hand, is a very complex character and I can see there is more to her than meets the eye – she is a very possessive, impulsive and compulsive person, eating disorders, complex issues and very bitter – it's a shame, there is a little girl inside that demonic mind.'

Friday 17th September 2004

'Not much exciting happening today, working as usual, piglets all okay, came in tonight to read the paper, and right across the centre page was an article by Mark Bycroft with a picture of Hannah, it was so nice to see a picture that reminded me of home – rang Mark at home to tell him about the article and how it made me feel and Jacob come on the phone and told me he loved me and missed me and can't wait till I come home from my new job – well, I just wanted to burst into tears, oh my poor little baby I just want to be home NOW!'

Monday 20th September 2004

'Well, what a shock I haven't written in my calendar all weekend, that's a good sign surely, only 9 more days to go now!

I was working all day Saturday feeding the litluns – Pongo is my definite favourite – if only I had somewhere to put him I would most definitely take him home. They are all feeding well and growing well things are looking good for them. Babbles is due to give birth today too, I only hope Mrs C calls me when she starts so I can watch my first piggy birth!

Had a good visit yesterday – the kids are all doing well, shattered because they had all stayed out the night – I think they are all in need of a little bit of TLC from mummy! Mark was looking good too, but also in need of kisses and cuddles from me – I think he feels the same way as me, I can't wait to get home, cuddle up and just spend time with my family.

Rang mum today and left a message as she wasn't there – I'll ring back tonight or tomorrow.

Had a chat over the farm today with Tracie, Sandra and Tee – it's amazing Tracie is going through exactly the same with her family as I am – except for the kids, her brother and mum have been interfering too much in trying to look after her house etc and the whole family is at war now – she's dreading going home! I'm okay about it all now, mums okay, if my sister wants to have the hump she can go off and sort out her life and her problems in her head, I am not going to worry about it, all I am going to concentrate on is building my life back up with my family and friends – if anyone chooses not to be a part of my life, then so be it, I've had enough.

April has got very clingy with me now so I will have to back off a little, she has opened up a lot to me and told me what happened, her step son died, he fell off the worktop in the kitchen and fractured his skull, but in court it came out that her partner at the time, the child's dad had been beating the child over a period of time and they both were charged with manslaughter. She has no contact with any of her children whatsoever, they have all been adopted elsewhere now, and she has no pictures whatsoever of any of them up which is a real shame – I am sure her children are missing her terribly but it seems like she has cut them out of her mind as that's the only way she can cope – she showed me a poem she had written to them titled 'regrets' – it really brought a tear to my eye, its addressed to her children but they have never seen it, or even know of its existence.

April expresses her emotion through drawings, she is a fantastic artist and gets lost in her own little world, but in another world she would make a great artist I am sure, perhaps one day she will fulfil that ambition'.

Tuesday 21st September 2004

'Well, what a day, went to work this morning, started feeding and then Babble gave birth to one piglet so everything stopped and we all watched and waited in anticipation – nothing! She grunted, groaned,

strained and farted for about 5 hours with us sitting there, urging her on, pushing for her, I think we have all come away with piles!

We gave up at lunchtime and came in for rolecall and lunch, I took my lunch outside, there she was still pushing, then I went and done some fencework and came back – another 3 piglets, all pink ones plus one dead one, so that was it, I sat with her and stayed there till another 2 came out but sadly they were both dead, Mr Botes said they had been dead a while so it wasn't because she had a long labour. I had to come in at 5pm for roll-call but apparently she went on to give birth to another two – this time alive thank goodness – what a day!

Rang Mark tonight, no news yet, only had £1.00 on my phone credit so I didn't speak to the kids, as soon as I put the phone down I got a tannoy to attend centre office – Mrs Carruthers said to me 'can you read and write?' – yes, then read this – I sat down and read 'you are being released on HDC – 28/9/04, that's this Tuesday – I wanted to scream, I couldn't stop saying thank you to Mrs Carruthers – I signed to accept and came out, I couldn't believe it, finally I could see an end, it was real, I was going home.

A strange feeling then came over me and I was dreading telling the girls in the dorm because I knew how they would feel – a lot of them aren't going home for a long time, it's not fair.

As I went into the dorm, Marlene came over and said congrats, she must have heard the news somehow, and with that they all came over and wanted to know what news. I told them all and Lorraine pointed at me with her finger and said 'come here, you', oh my god I thought I was in trouble now and she gave me the biggest hug ever and I just burst into tears – I just can't believe it's nearly over.

Then I wanted to ring Mark to tell him but I didn't have any credit left, its Tuesday nobody has any credit left on a Tuesday! I will have to ring him in the morning as soon as my credit goes on – watch out home, here I come!!!'

Wednesday 22nd September 2004

'Worked today, everyone now knows I am going home Tuesday – amazing grapevine here, who needs telephones! Wanted to ring Mark so much to tell him the news but I kept trying the phone just in case the credit had gone on, but in the end I couldn't get through until 4.30pm, when I told him he just sighed heavily, I think when he put the phone down he probably had a little cry to himself, just like I did. I am so excited now, with each hour I am getting even more excited, I keep looking round and thinking 'yes, at last'. Then I rang mum and told her, obviously she was glad it was nearly over for me.

I got a lovely letter today from Kate and Angela and Julian, so much support from people that you didn't know cared so much, if only they knew how much it all meant to me, so I done a letter back to them plus one to Sally. I got a letter from Stewart too so I sent him the news too, and I sent Greg a birthday card as I actually come out on his birthday and I have a feeling he is 50 this year!

Went to the church service in the evening which I found very emotional, we were talking about confronting issues and breaking down barriers – I think everyone in the room could relate to that as they each had their own issues to confront and barrier to break down. They were saying we take so much all our life and then something happens and we decide were not going to take it any more – that's God's way of guiding you down the right path – confront your demons and settle them – move on. I feel that although I have confronted my issues I know when I go home I will need to keep on confronting them until people realise I mean it, my wall is crumbling but I am determined to give it one last blow with the sledgehammer!'

Thursday 23rd September 2004

'Had a bad nights sleep last night, don't know why I just could not sleep, tossing and turning, covers off,

then on again. I think I will spend my day off asleep or at the very least laying on my bed relaxing.

Had a call from Centre Office today to ring Mark at home – talk about panic, I thought something had happened, I rang him and he was beside himself with worry – apparently the letter I wrote to the Daily Mail has just been published in today's newspaper! My reaction was 'Hey great' – his was 'great, what if they stop your HDC because of it?' I reassured him that they wouldn't do that – that they had seen the letter go out to the newspaper and hadn't stopped it and also it wasn't about any one person or place in particular, therefore nobody should get the hump, but just to reassure Mark I said I would rip the letters page out of all the newspapers here so nobody would see it, he was happy at that. I think he was just panicking, but anyway I went round and gathered up all the newspapers before anyone could read it, but I actually felt quite proud that it had been printed, it's a view of my experience of my time in the system – right or wrong, I felt it's important that other people know.'

Friday 24th September 2004

'Good day at work today, really busy, the day went quickly but I was so tired, didn't sleep again last night or the night before, Tracy said I've got 'gate fever', apparently well known – the week before you

go home you are tired, can't sleep, worried, scared etc etc.

Handed out most of my clothes off my prop card so that I can wear them out Sunday – we can't decide whether to do the zoo or Hastings, I had a look on the local 'whats on' and just round the corner there is a South of England Rare Breeds Centre, sounds like a bigger Godstone Farm, which might be fun for the kids (and me), but to be honest I don't care where we go but we must get a McDonalds!!!!!

I just so want this all over now.'

Sunday 26th September 2004

'Really rushed today, had breakfast, done my house job, had a shower and got ready for the day. Mark and the children picked me up and off we went – felt quite strange but not weird. We decided to go to the Rare Breeds Centre and it was a nice day, we all played on the marsh trail and it was good fun, and we even got a McDonalds on the way back!!!!

Jacob had been calling my name all day left, right and centre, desperate for attention. The other two weren't so bad but Jacob was just desperate for contact with me, he wouldn't take his eyes off me in case I disappeared. Felt strange to be with them all day, when I got back I just collapsed on the bed and wanted to sleep but I couldn't because my mind was racing.'

Monday 27th September 2004

'Can't believe it's my last day at work – I am so going to miss everyone here – including the pigs! Took biscuits over to have with tea break – we had a nice relaxed tea-break in the morning but in the afternoon all chaos let rip;

After lunch Mr B (Sir Chris as we girls all called him), said we would quickly get up Spud and Shannon (horses) as the vet was due at 2.30pm so off we set, me with Shannons head collar, Mr B with Spuds and Tracie carrying the food. Now we all know what a sod Spud can be and so it was decided that Mr B would take Spud as he is too much of a handful for us girlies and I would take Shannon – they were both okay getting their head collars on, Spud was a little anxious but okay (ish) walking across the field he was a nuisance, Shannon was fine, very aware of all around her and a bit nervous of Spud behind her, I became aware that he was rearing, kicking and circling all the time with Mr B kicking him back and using all his strength to control him.

When we got to the concrete road, Spud had overtaken us and by this time getting very stressed. Then the damned pigs squealed to say hi and that was it, Spud reared up in front of me, trying to stamp on Mr B, all the time reversing towards Shannon, whose ears by now were severely pointing backwards (not a good sign) and she had started jumping on her front legs (an even worse sign), trying to remain calm and in control I held on to Shannon speaking to her gently trying to calm her down when all of a sudden, I was squashed between Shannon, the brick wall and Spuds backside with his legs kicking, just as I thought this is it, my last day and I am going to die, I looked over and I saw him stamp on Mr B's chest and catch his face with his hoof, Mr B grabbed at his face, threw the rope at Spud and then within seconds there was blood everywhere. I could see that Spud was going to trample all of us with Shannon in the way so I turned Shannon round and pointed her towards the field and let go of her rope and they both ran off, bolting across the field.

Me and Tracy calmly but quickly took Mr B to Healthcare, his face split open, he was holding his chin together with his hand, they took over instantly, cleaned him up and sent him to hospital to be stitched back up again and checked over.

Me and Tracy made our way back to the farm, we were in absolute shock, we knew Spud was a psycho and unpredictable and could only think how glad we was that it wasn't one of us holding Spud, can you imagine that. Would you believe it would happen the one day there is only 2 people on the farm, usually there is at least 4 staff. We set off to find Mr & Mrs C (farm managers) and they were at home sorting out their cellar, just as the same time the vet turned up, life had to go on as normal and the pigs needed to be swabbed. So in we went, me and Tracy, still in shock, we now had to tackle a pen full of approximately 30 pigs. We decided the only way to tackle them was to literally rugby tackle them and jump on them and hope you grab the ears of the right one, well we have never giggled so much, we were all over the place, jumping from one pig to another, wrapping our legs round them, sitting on them, catching them in between our legs and being dragged along holding onto their ears at one point!! Even Mrs C couldn't stop laughing and it made her smile after an awful day, but we got them all – she couldn't stop saying 'well done' to both of us for getting stuck in.

After this, we had to move 3 pigs from one pen to another extremely quickly as Spud (who they had managed to catch and put in a pen) was waiting to go into the other pen to be held there until they decided if he was going to be moved on to another farm or not, following the incident.

We looked at each other and decided without saying anything that the only way to get these pigs quickly was to rugby tackle them and lift them up by the legs, I got the front and Tracy got the back and we literally threw them into the other pen one by one – there was flying pigs today that's for sure.

I finally finished work about 5pm, after a tearful goodbye to everyone, I assured them all I would never forget today. Back in the dorm we had a giggle tonight too, I handed out all my excesses (milky way, coffee, refreshers, frosties, shampoo etc) all the luxuries that are scarce to get in here but so welcome, and then we all sat telling stories, we all thought we had good stories until Karinna started talking – what that girl has seen is most definitely not what a girl of 24 should have seen that's for sure. She has sat and watched her friends perform in a porn show, over and over again, common place to her! Gobsmacked we were, I can tell you, what a night!'

Just as a note, a few years later Tracy was released and bought a batch of piglets from the farm. She started her own pig farm with them. I'm very proud of her and all she achieved, so much so that she was awarded Barclays Business Person of the year some years after being released and becoming a very successful pig farmer – well done Tracy!

Tuesday 28th September 2004

'Home today – it only sank in yesterday that I am going home today but boy do I know it this morning!

Got up so early I could not sleep, had a shower, went down for breakfast with Tee and said my goodbyes to everyone – I didn't cry, I was just so excited about going home. Sandra was the only one who brought tears to my eyes – if only I could take her with me.

Checked out of my bedspace then I had to sit and wait, I was looking out of my window, it was 9.10am, just as I was wondering why did I tell him to pick me up at 10, I saw my car pull up and rushed my stuff down to reception, by the time I got out it was 9.50am. I walked out, did not look back and got in my car and said, 'Take me home honey.' Home we went.'

Reading this back now, it seems there was so much going on that I didn't even realise all the girls from the dorm had gone off to work because nobody likes to say goodbye in places like this. It reminds them they are still here, if that makes sense.

The reason I didn't look back was, as they say, that if you look back as you leave, you will return.

The sadness of leaving Sandra in there was immense. She had served almost 15 years for killing her violent husband, yet she was the gentlest woman you could ever meet. She shouldn't have been there. She should be at home with her daughter now, trying to rebuild what she has left of her life, but because she refuses to say sorry for her crime, they do not entitle her to parole. You tell me where the justice in that is.

I realised quickly too that Mark had a hostage in the car's boot - one chicken from the farm that Mrs C had given me as a reminder of my time here - we called him Papillon because he was one escapee.

I can still remember the feeling of coming home. The children were at school. I got out of the car and the dog came running up to me. My mum was waiting outside and had brought me some flowers, but then she left. I didn't understand why she wouldn't come in for a cup of tea. I had been in a cocoon and had not seen what had been going on in the outside world, but now I was about to learn it all, whether or not I liked it.

I know there are always two sides to a story and soon it became apparent this was the case. One side Mark saw where, according to him, all he was worried about was me and the children. Then there was the other side from my mum and sister. When I was inside, they said they had done their best to look after the children, but Mark had made it impossible and was rude to them. They had walked away and left my children with no mum, no aunty, and no nanny.

Despite their reasons, this had a devastating effect on my children, not as devastating as losing their mum, but it just reinforced the fact there was nobody for them to talk to or to turn to, apart from Mark. A very difficult time for all, with long-lasting anger from all sides that would take many years to repair, but for some irreparable.

I don't think I ever understood the damage that had been done to my children. The separation that had been forced on them all, from me being taken away because of something they didn't understand, to the shame that it had brought on them. Their friends knowing has really affected them over the years, plus the upset at home. I know they felt abandoned when they found out that my sister and my mum had gone on holiday with my sister's children, but left them behind. This is something they have never talked about and I haven't talked about either. It is too painful a memory that I cannot change or address, whether that's right or wrong.

I suppose you could say that's part of my reason for writing this book. It is my way of letting my children know what happened and how I felt about leaving them. Without sitting down, talking with them and bringing back the pain and bad feeling, this is my closure and acknowledgement of that time. I hope it brings an end and acceptance to all my family too, but for now here is a picture of the one true escapee, Papillon!

Part 3

NOW FOR THE NEXT CHAPTER

Life wasn't easy to start again. I was home and that seemed the best thing on this planet, but there was so much more to take on board. This was just the tip of the iceberg.

The children had been through so much and I didn't know how to approach what happened with them. I couldn't even speak about my own experience. All I could do was be there for them and hug them.

Things have been difficult between the family members with everything that went on when I was away, it's not been repaired and not been forgotten so it's been boiling inside of them all, like a deep cut leaving a scar to remind you how bad it was.

It's been nearly five months since I came home. I haven't been able to talk about my experience to anyone except the computer, for many reasons. The people closest to me struggle. I don't want to see them upset anymore; my family doesn't want to acknowledge what has happened, therefore they don't want to hear when I want to talk. My friends will happily sit and listen, but how far does it go? Do they really realise what it means? I wish I could make them all feel how I felt so that they truly appreciate what it has made me become and how it has changed me as a person.

Tonight, for instance, there was a programme on TV; a drama based on real-life. It is the story of a mum who was jailed for life for the murder of her two babies. I know from history that she was freed on appeal, but the programme was the story about how she got there. I think it was the hardest thing I've ever had to watch since being out because it was so real, but watch it, I had to. I had to know that other people felt the same way as I did when I first went in and what it was like. The programme researchers carried out their work with immaculate documentation and it was very real to watch, so real in fact if I had changed the charges, it could well have been me.

The programme paused for the news, so I went downstairs to make tea for the break only to find Mark laying on the front room floor absolutely sobbing. As sad as that is, the saddest thing was that I didn't know what to say to him. I couldn't comfort him. I couldn't tell him it would be alright. I couldn't say, 'Don't worry.' All I could do was sit with him rubbing his back as he cried. You see, he has his own demons to fight. He feels that he wasn't there for me, to protect me, his little baby girl, and he couldn't help me and take away all this pain. Not just for me but for all of us.

We have tried to talk about what has happened, but it seems to end the same way. He cannot listen to my stories because the guilt upsets him and as a result, I cannot tell him my stories because I do not want to hurt him all over again. But by the same token, I cannot sit and listen to his stories of when I wasn't here because I get so upset, racked by the guilt of a mother who was not there for her children.

He went to bed, and I sat downstairs watching the second part, which told the story of her appeal and her eventual release. Then the programme ended, I asked the TV, 'But what then?'

Nobody has ever covered the feelings of when you are first released. The euphoric feeling of not believing you are going home. Prison makes a person feel that regardless of their sentence or crime, they will never leave the prison walls. In my experience, I felt that something would happen, and I would end my days there, never to see the children again and them not knowing how I felt. You never really believe it will one day be over. In reality, that day comes for most people, but the memory of the ordeal will last forever.

Arriving home, you want to touch the walls of the house, experience the feel of the grass, the smell of the washing; all these things that we all take for granted every day. I was desperate to vacuum the front room. How desperate is that? Just the normal household things my time away had deprived me of that I needed to fulfil.

Then, of course, there is the guilt. Not the obvious guilt of your crime and the reality of what you have done, because that hits home before they sentence you, but there's the guilt of being free. Most people do not understand why I feel guilty about sitting here at home telling the computer what I feel. I am reminded of those people I have met, good and bad. I am out here, and they are still in there. In most cases, they all have their story to tell for whatever reason. Some have a small amount of time left to serve and you feel glad for them but sad as well because their life when they come out will never be the same as before they went in. Sometimes, this is a blessing because the life they were leading led them to do what they did, and they can only come out to better things and more hope for a future. But for others, where you have to question the justice of the sentence, it ruined their lives. Their children have grown up, their homes lost, husbands abandoned them and they are too old to start again. Thinking of them, you question who is right and who is wrong. The people who admit to a crime, occasionally justify their reasons for committing it in the first place, but still, they are sentenced without sympathy, as if the authorities couldn't give a damn. Where is the reasoning?

In the early days after coming home, I struggled to go out of the house. I didn't know how to dress in public because I thought everyone was looking at me in disgust for what I had done. I felt so ashamed and, because I lived in a small close-knit village in a lovely community, how could I have done something so bad? Well, that's how I felt. Later, I learned that so many people were supporting me. Because of the person I was before, they knew that I had meant no badness from what I did. It was because of circumstances. I have never let those people know how much I appreciated their support. This feeling of shame continued for many years. I cried in private at what had happened, and I had no way of changing it or making it better for those that had suffered.

I guess I had a few weeks of trying to get myself operating as a mum again, picking Jacob up from school, being there after school for Rachel and Thomas, doing homework, and cooking dinner. It's a strange thing to say, but after four months inside, I had become institutionalised. I had become accustomed to having dinner cooked for me and then being locked in a room without the freedom to do all I wanted, go where I wanted, when I wanted. I enjoyed vacuuming the lounge because I could! Once, at about one in the morning, I sat in the garden in the darkness, nobody awake, nobody aware of where I was but I was grateful that I could do that. There was nobody I could speak to about it and how I felt. Because I had an electronic tag on for some weeks, I had to be home by nine o'clock every night, plus I had a weekly visit from probation. Others hadn't experienced these feelings and wouldn't understand how I felt, so I kept it all bottled inside. Good or bad, that's the only choice I had. Now and then, I tried to talk about it with certain people, but they didn't understand and didn't want to hear. I guess writing this book has become a way of getting my emotions out.

There's been a lot of anger, mostly between Mark, my sister, and my mum. It doesn't seem to be going anywhere soon either. The latest is that my mum has said she is selling the caravan; the one place of happiness that we could all escape to. I guess with the breakdown of all the relationships, those days are gone. The children are growing up and won't want to go to the caravan again; I guess time is moving on. We offered to buy the caravan from Mum to keep for the kids; they loved it but she sold it back to the site instead. It all turned nasty. My mum and sister both accused me of stealing the caravan rental money from them, but I stole nothing from them. I have never stolen from anyone in my life. I was made to feel like a criminal again. I took none of the rental money for myself. It all went on the caravan and to pay the fees, but I have never had the opportunity to explain myself. They had already made a decision against me and wrote to tell me what they thought of me and what they felt I had done. Time heals, but feelings remain.

I had lost my full-time career with the house building company and it was impossible to find employment again. As soon as I revealed what had happened to me, despite my experience or previous career, it made no difference. They closed the file and showed me the door. After a while, I went for small part-time jobs where they didn't ask about my experience or my history. It felt as though I had spent all these years getting experience, but had gone back to the start. My jobs brought in a little money, so I did whatever I had to do, cleaning, working in a shop, or serving tea and coffee in a café. It all helped not just pay the bills, but it got me used to dealing with people again and building up my confidence with the public. Slowly, I wiped away the branding I imagined was tattooed across my forehead; ex-convict.

I served in a little kitchenware shop for a while. No pressure, no aims or goals, and no ambition. Then the time came for me to build myself up again. I needed to make a difference, to do something that would make me proud, so I went for an administration job in a wealth management company and avoided the question about previous convictions. That all went well, and it introduced me back to working with computer systems and a professional life rather than shop life, dressing smart and being somebody that people respected. That was until I was called into the office one day. Somebody had made enquiries or someone snitched on me and told them I was an ex-convict. I tried to explain but it was no good. They had to let me go.

When I came home, the council was chasing me to pay back the money that I wrongly claimed. I am sure they think I never paid the rent at all, and I have a stash of money somewhere. How wrong can they be? Because I cannot pay back in one lump sum, they now want to make me bankrupt. The sense of it all is hard for me to see. I could not get a job because of this experience and have not been earning since they took me away from my employment and home. I have absolutely no income and they expect me to get a loan to repay them. Few money lenders I can think of where I would fit their criteria!

They do not want me to rebuild my damaged life or that of my family. Every time I seem to pull my head above the water, they push me back down again. How many times do you get pushed down before you don't bother lifting your head up again?

Well, rebuilding my life is exactly what I am doing. I am working again, albeit part-time. Some things are more important than money. Right now, I need to be a mum, have kids home for tea, pick kids up from school, and run them around all over the place, moaning like hell about doing so. You know, all the normal things a mum does.

* * *

I am now bankrupt, but still they keep trying. Trying to remind me constantly that they are watching me and they want their pound of flesh, like vultures hovering around a dying zebra. But now I have grown strong, I have seen weak people, and I have seen strong people and I know who I am. Yes, I have done wrong but I have paid and that should be the end. My lesson to all of you who think you can get away with any crime no matter what your reason is, don't be so stupid, appreciate the life you have. Yes, it's bloody hard work, and it never seems to pay to be honest, but you will be rewarded in this life or the next. Don't risk losing your family, your home, your life, your friends. Just be grateful for what you have, no matter how small it may seem. The world is still a beautiful place - you just have to believe it.

The motto is:
Life is short. Break the rules. Forgive quickly. Kiss slowly. Love truly. Laugh uncontrollably and never regret anything that made you smile.

Life may not be the party we hoped for, but while we're here we should dance.

So here I was again. How long was it going to be before I could prove myself a good person, a good person, and a good mum? Like a voice out of heaven, a friend of mine who knew what had happened and had supported me in prison rang me and said her boss was looking for an admin person in their estate agents. Would I like to go for an interview? YES!!!!!

The Boss, as I called him, was lovely, and I felt he knew where I had come from and what I was looking for. He gave me a chance on the team. I was so delighted; I had a chance for a new start and took it with open arms. To begin with, I was in admin and soon became a Trainee Negotiator; I fitted in with the team and nothing was mentioned about what I had been doing or where I had come from. There were a couple of people I confided in, so that I knew I wasn't trying to fool anyone or be deceitful. It felt the right thing to do.

Three years in this lovely company and I tried on my own as a Lettings Agent. Having gone from sales negotiator to lettings negotiator, I felt confident in all that I had learned and accomplished. With the support of The Boss and Mark, I launched my solo career from the garden shed at home – not an ideal location, but it was cheap!

I didn't realise, but The Boss was to become a lifelong friend and one I am still friends with today and proud to call my friend.

Five years on, I have now repaid the council a settlement of £36,000 but still have my bankruptcy on my credit rating. We have had to re-mortgage the property to pay back the council and life is a financial struggle. On another subject, because we had to re-mortgage, we cancelled the Deed of Trust, giving me fifty percent of the property, mainly as a way of protecting the property. That way the bankruptcy could not affect the property, but in doing so I had no way of protecting my share and I was to pay the price for this later. Mark said it wouldn't matter because once we were married, it would belong to both of us anyway, and I trusted him.

It was a tough choice. We had no actual income coming in regularly, but I was determined to make it work, to build it up into something that one day would benefit my children in a way that I never could. I was building up contacts within the property industry and having some tough conversations, one of which was when I was making a call to one of the top bods in Rightmove. While trying to negotiate a monthly fee for advertising my properties, he noticed something I hadn't considered. 'Is that a cockerel in your office?' Papillon had done his usual crowing to let me know someone was coming down the drive but I hadn't realised our conversation was in earshot of the garden shed. It was a sunny day, and the doors were open. 'That's all part of living in the country,' I said. I smiled and continued the conversation, as professional as ever.

It had been just over a year of running with my own thing. I had contacted one of the leading agents and was trying to convince them to take me on as their agent in this area. It was Christmas. She was considering it and would let me know in the new year. On New Year's Eve, she called me and offered me a full-time position as Property Manager covering the south Kent area. I didn't need her to finish the sentence before I accepted. I was so proud I had made it. So much time had passed that I no longer had to declare my previous convictions and I no longer felt the need to either. I had achieved what I had hoped for, respect and professional success. My career, which stopped in 2004, had now started again in 2010. Six long hard years of struggling for money, struggling for respect and to be a human again. Someone who could hold her head up high and say, 'I have achieved.' The feeling was good – Happy New Year!

The job was good. Working within a great team, I was looking after lovely houses far and wide, big and small, belonging to all sorts. From multi-millionaires, politicians, and celebrities to everyday people who could let out their homes for a while. My job was varied, and I was proud to say I could talk to all my customers regardless of who they were and what they had, this was where I used my experience of people to switch between classes and form one-to-one client/customer relationships. I can't name any of them for reasons of confidentiality, but let's say my phone contact list was very impressive!

Travel formed a big part of my day as I had to cover the southeast. My day was long and by the time I got home I was truly shattered, but I appreciated having the job, so I didn't care.

The company put me through the official training, so I had the perfect basis for my career. I had to travel to London regularly for updates and work in other branches, which was only a plus for my experience. The team that I was with were great and are all still friends today. We went through some hilarious times and some not-so-funny. We said we could write a book about being estate agents. That may be the next one I plan so watch this space! One experience I will always recall is going out to a large property in the deepest countryside because the tenant said the electric gates were stuck shut and he was trapped inside. He had to get his car out (the background to this was he was behind with his rent and was refusing us access to the property, so there were some issues. We wouldn't let him have the spare keys for the gates as part of the negotiations). It was office closing time and everyone had gone home apart from me. I agreed to go out with the spare keys to open the gate and let him out. When I eventually got there, no one was around and the place was in darkness. I got out of the car to look around and was sprung upon by his bodyguards who basically said I couldn't leave without handing the keys over. I guess you could say I was held to ransom. I tried to call the office, but nobody was there. Then I rang my director's mobile number and he said he would get in touch with the landlord of the property who called me back and said under no circumstances was I to hand the keys over. To cut a very long story short, if I didn't hand the keys over, I was going to disappear, so I had to part with them and drove home sobbing. A long court case ensued between the landlord and the tenant, but no further action was taken. I think that experience had taken its toll on my confidence but I didn't realise till years later.

I was at that company for a few years; the travelling was hard on me and I was looking elsewhere when a local company approached me and said they were thinking about starting a new lettings department within their company and would I be interested in starting it. Well, this was a big consideration. It was to be my own baby. I would be the only Lettings Manager of the new department starting completely from scratch, plus I wouldn't have the travelling. All they dealt in were local properties and the salary was on par but with the promise of a yearly bonus, dependent on how well I built the company up. I weighed up all the options and went for it, onwards and upwards.

I started with a desk and a computer in the back office and went from there. After the first year, I had done well and built up the managed properties to a respectful number.

The job was high-pressure, stressful, with long hours, but it was promising for the future and I was hopeful of building the department and adding more people, so it was a magnificent prospect. The team were nice apart from one pain-in-the-ass woman, but I've dealt with worse, so bring it on! I knew this woman was an issue after approximately a year. I saw her one day when she thought I couldn't see her; she was looking me up and down as if I was a piece of filth that she had trod on yet was as nice as she could be to my face. I soon got the measure of this two-faced person and from that day on I gave her the respect she deserved – none!

I am now established in my industry. Having given up working for myself, I have taken a role in a major estate agency and have earned letters after my name after studying for a professional diploma in my career. At fifty years old, I am settled in my career and probably have reached as far as I can go. I am now looking for alternatives for the last section of life when I should take it easier. It's called retirement!

I have been no angel. When I realised I would not be married to Mark, I questioned why I was in this relationship and where it was going. At about the same time, a friend from many years ago started texting me and we began chatting regularly, which led to more intense conversations. This ignited my spark for life and I felt like a giggly schoolgirl, wrongly I know, but I felt wanted. Nothing ever came of it, but it gave me hope that the right relationship was out there somewhere.

As a result, my relationship with Mark has broken down over the years. We are both hanging on mainly for our son, Jacob. The relationship between my other children and Mark has gone to where they do not feel comfortable coming to the house for Sunday lunch. This is devastating for me, but the choice is if I leave, my already damaged family will be spoiled more. If I leave, I can give the children somewhere to go, or I can stay and be near my son but grow further from my other children. It's such a hard decision and not one that anyone should ever have to make, which is why it has taken so long for me to get to this point that I feel there is no choice now. I am a mum first and I owe it to all my children to be there for them.

If I felt a little lost, I would get in my car and drive to my dad's, sit outside for a while contemplating life, and look at the garden, remembering how Dad used to sit on the front step while I would dig the garden. It was on one of these occasions when suddenly I realised there was a lady sitting on the front step watching her children play in the front garden. It made me smile; history was repeating itself in a good way. Then I saw her young daughter come running up to her for a cuddle and she was the image of a young me. Long blonde hair, about seven years old. It was the first time for a long time, that I had driven to my dad's and smiled at the memory, time was passing, the sadness was changing. I was remembering the good times.

The lady saw me sitting in the car and beckoned me over. As much as I wanted the ground to swallow me up, I sat there looking at her house. Suddenly I felt like a stalker! I had no option but to get out of the car and go over. I felt like someone had caught me out, but I thought there's no way out of it, just explain. So I did. She invited me in to look around (which I politely refused) but her children came and said hello and told me of the things they had found in the garden. Things that we had put there when we were young, my Mynah bird's stone (Jim) that my brother engraved when the bird died and was laid to rest under the sycamore tree in the garden. I told the children stories of when I was young and they listened, eyes wide, taking it all in. The boy said he would lay some flowers on Jim's grave and always remember the bird, bless him. With that, I said how good it had been to see such a lovely family in there and left with a smile – time to move on.

* * *

I have since left the house twice and gone into a private rental. My mistake from a long time ago was not putting my name on the deeds of the house. Mark is now refusing to buy me out fairly so that I can try to rebuild my life. He is adamant that the amount we had to re-mortgage to repay the bankruptcy will be deducted from my share of the profit from the house. He now thinks he had no role in the debt. The first time I went back thinking we had made a terrible mistake, only to be assured three months later I do not belong there anymore. The second time I left, I found a private tenancy and was happy there. Unfortunately, it only lasted for six months until the landlord came back. Then I was officially homeless for two months, sleeping on the sofa of my eighty-year-old mother's and part-time in my sister's spare bedroom - not seeing any of the children. The council didn't want to know as I was working full time; I spiralled into a deep depression and ended up going back to Mark. I think we both now realise I am only there as I have nowhere else and until the house sells so that we can separate financially and emotionally; we are both stuck.

It was during one of these moments when I realised that our relationship has suffered beyond repair and although I truly think we still love each other; we have become trapped and don't know how to make it good again. He is living his life and doing all he can for himself and our son. He excludes me completely and I go about my life doing what I must to make sense of it all. Then one evening at home, I was quietly sitting in the lounge contemplating life. What were my hopes? What difference was I aiming for this year? What did I want to achieve now? Too many questions to answer, so I picked up my iPad and went on Facebook for a catch-up. One of my friends was selling her chicken coop. Did I need a new one? – no. One of my other friends was arranging a games night. Was I interested? – maybe. But my niece was doing a charity run for one of her friends and she was trying to raise funds. If I clicked on the line, I would donate £10. As I was sitting there not doing anything, I clicked on the charity. It made me feel good to donate. It was for breast cancer which my dad's mum died from when she was thirty-six, and my dad had idolised the mum he had lost at such a young age. He never really talked about her much, but I know he would beam with pride at the thought of helping others who were facing this terrible disease. I thought it looked interesting.

Before I knew it, I was looking into the challenges people can take part in and, as I was scrolling through the various Mud Runs, it moved on to international challenges and Cycle

Africa hit me. Click here for more information; that was me engrossed. The site told about cycling across Tanzania, across the Serengeti, camping with the Maasai under the galaxy of stars. I was hooked and before I knew it I had clicked sign me up and paid £300. Oops, better shut the iPad now and go to bed!

Africa was a place I had always wanted to go to but knew I could never afford it. Also, I would never have had the confidence to go on a holiday like that on my own. But this way, I would do it for a great cause, Women v Cancer Charity, and it would be a wonderful challenge to take on in my fiftieth year, to prove that I am a strong woman who can make a difference.

It seemed a good idea, exciting, life-changing, and challenging. I could be proud of doing something good; giving rather than taking. Then the realisation of having to raise over £3,000 in fundraising and cycling 400 km across Africa on my own suddenly sunk in and panic took over!

No time for panic, exercise regime to work out and ideas for fundraising started!

Okay, I woke up to the stark reality of what I had signed up for, raising £3,000 for the charity before I could go. I had to let everyone know.

I think it's fair to say that I have put all my efforts and concentration into the challenge and focused on this rather than my failed relationship. Having to work out how to fundraise takes my mind away from having to work out what I should do in my relationship to either make it better or end it.

Anyway, training had to start, so I immediately went to Halfords and bought a £200 hybrid bike, thinking I was now professional, but forgetting there was one minor item of actually getting on it and cycling to consider. Oops!

I firmly remember the first day of cycling training. I thought I would just go round the village and back to get my cycling legs, didn't realise there was a slight incline so I did less than two miles. The only thing that got me home was the idea of putting my feet up, my bum was sore, my legs ached and I was puffing like a steam train but I got home and all I thought was, How the heck am I going to do 250 miles when I can't manage two miles? Needless to say, there followed a regime of every weekend training and I felt by the time I could easily do a twenty-mile round trip, I had got it in the hat. Sometimes I found a cycling buddy to go out with, but often I got on my bike and went off on my own, usually finding circular routes that would end up back home and covering twenty to thirty miles.

I had just over a year to raise the money. First, I had to tell the family what madness I had agreed to. They were shocked but supportive. I had to explain to my work I was going to be taking time off and then I had to work out how I was going to think about raising that kind of money.

There followed a year of fundraising. Everything I did was to raise money, from Easter egg competitions, dressing stupid and going round with a bucket, cycling all day on a standstill bike outside my office with a pink tutu on and a bucket by the side of the bike, quiz nights up the local pub, disco nights at the local club, scrambling around for things to sell at boot sales (much to the kid's disgust when they realised I was selling all their old clothes). All the funds went to the charity, and it was so close. I had enjoyed every moment and met some wonderful people along the way. People I met shaking a bucket in a pub ended up having a heart-to-heart with me where both of us ended up crying into the bucket. I have heard some moving stories of survival, loss, recovery, and discovery from people that cancer has hit and the people that love them and have lost them. Then I had a cheque from Richard Stilgoe as he had heard what I was doing, and the local newspaper did an article on my fundraising, and this pushed me on further. I was so blown away by everyone's support it felt like I was doing good after all these years of trying to prove I was not a bad person. It made me feel it all had been worth it; I was giving back something to somebody, somewhere.

Then there was the training weekend with the charity, which was a fantastic introduction to everyone else who had signed up for the event. We had to share rooms with people we didn't know, which got us over that barrier, and the training up and down hills pushed us to levels that we didn't know we had, but we did it all the same. It was on this training weekend I found my lifelong cycling buddy Myfanwy, a Welsh girl of similar age. We developed a friendship that has given us both more than we could ever have imagined. We reached times of tears and nervous exhaustion, but we supported each other through thick and thin and remain firm friends years later.

In the training rides we did, we covered huge mileage and went up hills. I couldn't even walk up, let alone cycle up. I used to go red, struggling to breathe and thought I was unfit. It wasn't until years later that I questioned whether there may have been another reason I felt I was going to pass out at the top of each hill.

There were times when I doubted what I was doing and why. I had always been shy until I was about sixteen and then I had come out of my shell. I was still shy, but I realised if I didn't make any effort I wouldn't be included in anything, so I kind of put on a mask and pretended I was outgoing and lively. It was easier than being an awkward teenager who wanted to cry whenever someone talked to her, who would ever believe that my mask had held up so long and that I could take on something so adventurous, and on my own!

But we had done it. The time had come for our journey; I had got the kit together, and I was again leaving the children and Mark, but this time for a good reason and one that I had chosen. They were very proud of me for doing it; it was a turning point for me physically and mentally because I had done nothing like this before in my life. I wasn't adventurous; I was introverted but here I was, about to enter a period of life where I had to share a tent with a stranger, pee in front of everyone, and eat beans out of a can hoping a lion would not come out of the bushes!

After sharing a glass of prosecco with the girls and a wave to the family, we were gone and boarded the plane. Next stop Kenya.

Part 4

THE CYCLE DIARIES

The day had come. All our preparations and training were over, and now it was time to put it to the test. We met at Heathrow Airport. Some of us had only met once at the training weekend and we became known as The Glue Crew. A few others like us formed a small group. We were going to stick together in groups through it all, or that was the idea at least.

We said our farewells to our families and went through to departures. This was the start of our journey. Each and every one of us had our own personal reasons for doing this, but there was no going back now. We headed straight to the Sky Lounge for a glass of champagne and the first part of our journey to Africa, the first stop Kenya!

I have taken these diary entries from the diary that I took with me and wrote in every night to end the day and added a photo of the day to give you an idea of what life was like out there.

TRAVELLING DAY

Monday 19th October 2015

The coach trip across Kenya to the border was interesting to say the least - coming out of Nairobi the roads were cluttered with people, goats, donkeys and bikes, lots of shanty towns, people sitting around cooking at the side of the road, but all looking quite happy with their pot of something cooking amidst the dry, dusty soil.

After approximately 4 hours we reached the border which was swamped with jewelled women trying to sell their goods. At some point the border control felt quite intimidating, having to go through Kenya border first and scrutinized for Ebola and Yellow Fever by scanning your eyeball without blinking, quite scary especially when you're being stared at by a huge guy in uniform and not a smile in sight! Then you had to walk across the road to Tanzania dodging all the guys and women trying to sell you something very forcibly, to do it all again!

The scenery from the coach was amazing, going from Nairobi and slowly developing into the Africa you can only imagine, leaving the villages and entering the amazing scenery of the African land. Once over the border there was miles of dusty bush, every now and then a herd of goats and a shepherd, miles from anywhere or so it seemed. Donkeys wandering in the road with very few and far between cows who don't look like they have been well fed and not very stocky, not like UK grass-eating cows more like Ox with skin hanging on their bones and nibbling at dust. All the shepherds are dressed in traditional African robes.

A common sight out here is trees with 'bubbles' of nests hanging down from their branches with stories of how they got there, beautiful little yellow birds.

We had a packed lunch on the bus of boiled egg, very strange looking chicken leg with no meat on, fruit juice, bun and a hot dog sausage – a taste of what's to come!

Day 1 of cycling Moshi to Olpopongi Maasai village
Tuesday 20th October 2015, 84km

After a lovely sleep in the lodges, up at 5am for breakfast, debrief and load our bikes ready to set off by 6.30am. Still dark, but already warm, we are all feeling shattered from the travelling since Sunday evening, however our enthusiasm and excitement pushes us on and following a much needed warm up by Helen, we all get to our bikes for the start. Surprisingly feeling quite nervous, we set off on the off-road track down to Moshi where we join the Tarmac road and proceed through the town to lots of cheers and beeping, by now we are being driven by excitement and nerves all rolled into one.

Unfortunately for one of the girls it was at this point that just behind me I heard the clash of metal and realised that somebody had fallen in the group, we were all bunched together which made it difficult to stop without causing further collisions but we later learned that she had in fact broken her arm and had to be taken to hospital, after all that training and fundraising her ride was over, it was a stark realisation that it could have been anyone and we all felt for the unlucky lady that day.

The rest of the morning went well and by all accounts our speeds were good, making it to our first lunch stop at 10.30am of spaghetti Bolognese and fruit, the heat was now beginning to build up and the afternoons ride became much harder as the temperature rose, we then had to ride 20km off-road on a bumpy track to the Olpopongi Maasai village across the plains of Africa, arriving filthy dirty looking like we all had black stockings on!

Today for me became wee wall day! I had been using my water bottle instead of camelback and hadn't drunk enough water at all; I was beginning to feel badly dehydrated and got a bad stitch that I couldn't get rid of, then I really needed a wee and couldn't keep cycling so the girls had the brilliant idea of creating a wee wall around me so that I could squat and have a wee and carry on… only problem was we were in the middle of the high street and being watched by the entire population! Stupidly, I didn't realise everyone could see my white arse through their legs, but I didn't care. I desperately needed to wee, but then discovered I couldn't go as I had no water left in me to do a wee! I had to take time out on the bus and drink 2 litres of water before I was allowed to carry on…. hilarious after the event, especially when I found out one of the girls had taken a selfie with me squatting!

All along the route children were at the side of the road waving and calling out, 'Jambo'… there is a lot of poverty in Africa but I have never seen so many smiling happy faces, as we crossed the off-road track, in the distance were Impala and zebra with the occasional monkey, somebody said they saw giraffes in the distance but unfortunately not us!

Arriving at the Maasai village we were greeted by them doing a dance for us which was fabulous, we had to keep pinching ourselves to realise where we actually were, we then found our way to our little 2 man tents to get clean and changed ready for beer and dinner, peeling off our trousers this was when we realised how dirty we actually were as it looked like we had black stockings on with white socks and flip-flops!

A very welcome shower and flushing toilets were waiting for us, how they get flushing toilets and hot showers in the Maasai village is still a point of wonder and amazement to me, but I was extremely grateful for them!

That night after purchasing some trinkets from the Maasai we all sat round the campfire and had dinner and songs and a bottle of Kilimanjaro lager, before settling down for the night guarded by the Maasai. The occasional tree was carried in by the Maasai to restock the fire… no logs out here! Bloody amazing day, what a start.

Day 2 of cycling Olpopongi village to Arusha
Wednesday 21st October 2015, 84km

What a friggin day! We were up at 5am at the Maasai village, the reward for such an early start was an amazing view of the sky at night and all the galaxy's that are visible when there is no light pollution around, amazing.

Today ride we knew was going to be quite tough starting with 34km off-road, followed by 17km uphill and then 33km Tarmac road down to Arusha - simple!

We started off on the off-road which turned out to be sand and rock, at some points the sand was so deep it was impossible to cycle through and you had no choice other than to get off and walk… do you have any idea how hard it actually is to push a bike in sand and not to mention scary as every time you hit sand you felt like you had hit a brick wall and it took all your energy to stay on the bike. As the road went on it was made more difficult as we discovered the recent monsoon had actually washed away the existing road and blown the deep sand over the crevices… great! Needless to say I came off quite dramatically and scraped my arm and knee but got back on, and carried on… I think we eventually gave in and saw the funny side of it especially when a couple of the girls tried to keep cycling through the sand despite being thrown off at every opportunity – just like playing sand castles with our bikes really! As you can imagine, didn't take long for us all to be covered in dirt and sand yet again eventually a few of us drained of energy got on the bus having made the decision to save ourselves for the uphill rather than walking through the sand and depleting all our energy.

This part of the challenge proved to be the most challenging part for all of us, with even the hard core cyclists amongst us finding it difficult, taking approximately 5 hours to cycle this section alone. At the end of the sand tracks was our first fruit stop where we rejoined the group ready for the 17km uphill… I still don't know how some of the girls completed both these parts, it was tough, the hill just went on relentless the final portion of the hill I was crying as I reached the summit praying for the sight of the lunch tent and yes there it was… hallelujah!

After lunch we had a smooth 34km down to Arusha, cycling past a hyena and a monkey, both roadkill! Cycling into Arusha we realised we must have hit rush hour and it was very scary indeed, we all made sure we kept close together and concentrated on staying on the road despite the crazy African drivers, eventually we reached The Impala Hotel at Arusha, a very welcome sight which meant we would sleep tonight.

Day 3 of cycling Arusha to Zion campsite Tarangireti National Park
Thursday 22nd October 2015, 106km

Up at 5am again for an early start but at least we have had a good night's sleep in the hotel, not sure we will be able to say the same for tonight!

Today would be the longest day but the bonus was that the roads are all Tarmac and mostly undulating, we soon discovered the faster you go downhill the more speed to get up the other side without changing gear, another bonus was that we had cloud cover his morning which made cycling much easier the first 25km went in a flash and we were at our first fruit stop, then set off on our way to our lunch stop at Mtimmoja School, to be met by the whole school singing to us as we pulled in. This was absolutely magical, we had all brought gifts for the school of various useful items from school pens, pencils, colouring books to football net and footballs, toothbrushes and cuddly toys. After their singing we all sang back to them 'all things bright and beautiful' which went down very well and left us all in tears.

All of us then gave out all the items to the children, I have never seen a child look so pleased with his gift of a toothbrush, with a smile wider than you can imagine that I haven't seen for many Christmases then running off to a corner before somebody could take it off of them... we all felt we should have brought more with us and vowed to send out packages of uniforms, flip-flops and sports equipment. One of the little boys got a cuddly toy that someone had taken out there and he was so pleased with himself for getting it and then ran, but not before I got a photo! Some of the girls set up the football net and started to play football with the older ones whilst we took photos of the younger ones who were amazed at our cameras and all wanted to see the photos as soon as we had taken them, such a lovely sight to see these beautiful kids walking around with their football shirts on in all different sizes but they didn't care, they were proud but not as proud as us girls… A memory I will always cherish

After lunch we said a sad farewell to the school and hit the road again, stopping at the local village to spend our shillings, I had spent mine before I even got in the shop doing a deal with one of the looky looky men for a couple of t-shirts and then some bangles from the ladies, finally got in the shop for a coke and we were soon surrounded by the looky looky men, at one point one of the girls disappeared underneath a crowd of them trying to entice us with her goods and it was only when they started going that we realised she was still there, stuck underneath them all and all their baskets… A funny moment

After bartering and lots of banter with the locals we all got back on our bikes and headed to our camp for the night, the last 6km was very hard, the temperature had risen and we were all exhausted by the end and grateful for the day to be over.

The camp was quite basic but okay, we had toilets, beer and showers - what more do you need! More shopping in the camp shop followed by dinner by torchlight, the crew then surprised us by doing a song and dance for us all, which we promptly got up and danced with them, didn't want to go to our tents but by the end of the evening we were all shattered again and so to bed……not much sleep as in tents, quite uncomfortable plus listening to the hyenas through the night was something else…..seems we were guarded all night by Maasai around the campsite…how reassuring! A great night but not much sleep - best day for me so far, lots of lovely memories and experiences that I could not dream would be possible and will stay with me forever.

Day 4 of cycling Tarangire National Park to MtoWaMbu Lake Manyara National Park
Friday 23rd October 2015, 84 km

After a night at camp with not much sleep it was a struggle to get up this morning at 5am again, breakfast warm up and we were ready for the off, another 80km plus day…

The day started lovely with slight cloud making it cooler to cycle in, 40km of Tarmac road with slight inclines followed by 40km off-road.

The flat Tarmac road was fine and, I hate to say it, a little boring in parts as it was the main road and quite flat where you could see for miles, made a nice change though from previous days riding I guess.... We were passing through quite a few villages that seemed to be quite busy and for the first time a little intimidating so we were keen to pass through, eventually we turned off the Tarmac road and onto the off-road section, we pulled up for a fruit stop and then started the fun section...

The off-road although quite bumpy was fine and quite enjoyable, the scenery became much more lush with lots of vegetation as we entered the plantation at the base of Kilimanjaro with sugar beet fields on one side and cotton fields on the other, we were constantly being passed by local farmers on bikes with wide loads of freshly picked sugar canes, beautiful scenery mango trees and avocado trees... then we heard a rustling to the side of us and a Columbus monkey shot across our path to he delights of the girls... Our first wild animal!

We all stopped for lunch at a local farm which was absolutely delicious, all the time being observed by the local villagers all sitting watching us. After lunch back on the bikes for the hill which was short but steep followed by a dodgy downhill on rough ground with lots of sand at the bottom.... the dreaded sand!

At the bottom of the hill as we all came over the bridge we were met by the schoolchildren from the second school we were stopping at and a fruit stop, we all sneaked round to the kids much to their absolute delight!

We had saved a bag of goodies for this school too and they were delighted with this, the head teacher telling us that the government only provides a certain number of books per year and they have no fresh drinking water… quite an eye opener. The kids greeted us with singing and a boy was playing a drum of a bucket and stick nut my god what talent they all had, amazing wish we had brought a drum set with us for him!

After the school we were back on the bumpy track with a warning that it would get worse with more sand in places, and by God they were right! The road turned into a tractor track that was so uneven it took all your concentration to hold on for dear life whilst being shaken so much I got a headaches from my teeth rattling and my hat shaking against my head, it was truly horrendous and I didn't think I was going to make it. The temperature had also risen and it was as much as I could do to focus on just getting to the end, I felt like an emotional wreck where I was hanging on for dear life and thank goodness the girls with me were pushing me on at this point, for some reason I had scared myself stupid at this point of falling off and when we eventually pulled up to the finish line I burst into tears. Luckily the bus was there at the finish to take us all back to Twiga Lodge where we would be staying for 2 nights.

Believe it or not, the bus we got on then proceeded to break down, just as we were all knackered and just wanted to get back, however we did have all the staff on board and it promptly turned into the party bus singing and laughing, we had to pull up at a village so the guys could sort it out and before we knew it the looky looky ladies were reaching in with bracelets and baskets trying to sell them to us… it was hilarious and yes, we came home with baskets!

Back at Twiga, the rooms were quite basic but comfortable and we could at least have a shower so we didn't care, one of the girls announced the next morning they had a black mamba snake in their room which had to got rid of… apparently deadly, no antidote and a 15 minute fatal bite! Happy days.

Day 5 of cycling Mto Wa Mbu to Ngorongoro Crater Conservation Area
Saturday 24th October 2015, 44km

Well today is officially the shortest distance but the highest climb and the final day of cycling.

Our bodies are all exhausted from each day's challenging ride plus the travelling, lack of sleep from camping, and coping with the food adapting to the same food over and over again, cramping stomachs and dodgy tummies!

We spent last night at Twiga Lodge and are back there again tonight so at least we can actually say no more camping and we don't need to pack our bag again tonight, it's amazing how quick you adapt to living out of a bag!

Today we were split into 2 equal groups – group 1 that were doing both sections of today ride which incorporated the first section 17km of steep incline and then the next section of 27km of steep hills and declines up to the crater entrance… I had already decided that for me it was group 2 if I wanted to actually finish this in one piece without collapsing! Deep respect to group 1 for being able to do the whole thing but I knew that I was pushing myself to the extreme as it was so it was the right decision for me… in hindsight if I had my time again I would have gone with group 1…

Group 1 set off and about 20 minutes later group 2 got on the bus to the first stop to meet up with group 1- as we were chugging up the hill I honestly couldn't believe anyone could have cycled up that goddamn hill, it was amazing views with the Serengeti to the left and the Maasai mara to the right with sun dawning but at an incline of 14% I was glad I was not attempting it but had utter respect for those that had. For what seemed like ages, the bus kept chugging up the hill as it wound around hairpin bends to the point that we were all thinking we had come a different way as there is no way the girls have cycled up here… when suddenly we took another hairpin bend and there they all were at their water stop… to say we were all hanging out the windows cheering them on is an understatement, they had done it, bloody amazing each and every one of them!

When we got to our stop we all got off, waited for our bikes to follow us up in the van then set off on the final leg of the challenge. We were now quite high up the crater and the weather had changed, the higher we climbed you could feel the air getting thinner, the temperature cooler and clouds forming which was quite refreshing, however each slight incline felt like a huge hill as you couldn't get your breath as easily with the thin air, there was even a point going on a flat that it felt like hard work pedalling just to keep going. Each hill we noticed recovery at the top was not as easy as before as your lungs couldn't refill quick enough for the next dip and rise but we plodded on regardless taking each hill at a time, I don't think my gears actually came out of 1-3 at any time!

The benefit of these steep inclines was a number of very fast and very long declines, one of them we notched up 34 mph going downhill and almost overtook the crew on the motorbike! One memorable decline was so fast it actually was quite scary we were going so fast, couldn't brake as it was too steep and also you needed the speed to get you up the other side… there was one point that I could feel the wheels wobbling beneath me and I started to think 'if one of us comes off going down here it's all over' and when you start thinking at it becomes dangerous so you have to put it out if your mind and just go for it regardless.

We passed through several villages, we had locals whizzing past us on their bikes, completely taking no notice of the thin air or scary hills, no brakes on their bikes at all, no gears and definitely no gel saddles or padded trousers! Some of them had bags of corn on their backs, some with wide loads of sugar beet or banana leaf all strapped on their back of the bike with what looked like no effort at all. All the way through the villagers would call out to us 'pole pole' (pronounced poorly poorly meaning slowly slowly).

After approximately 21km of hills we realised that we must nearly be at the end and group 1 hadn't taken over us yet which meant we were actually at the front for the first time ever… the excitement of that gave us some renewed energy for the final push… until we came round the bottom of the final bend and saw the final hill in front of us… what a bugger it was, checking the gears were in the lowest gear we just hit the hill with determination to finish and by god, it took every ounce of determination and pulling thoughts of loved ones from the depths of your soul to push you up there. At some point I remember not thinking my legs are moving but I am just not going anywhere, it was at this point I actually looked up and looked around me and I was in complete awe of where I was, I was on the top of Africa with the Serengeti around me poking through the clouds, the air was so thin because we were so high up, for me I was seeing this beautiful country for my Dad and he was seeing what I was doing through my eyes, he knew I could make it and I felt I had to prove it to myself that I could do this, he had made me strong in life to deal with all that it had to throw at me and I was strong enough to do this, needless to say I was crying by now…

Shortly after I realised that I was flanked each side by 2 local children on bikes, one pushing and one weaving across the road pushing me on to finish. As I approached the top I could just make out somebody there with the magi men and realised it was one of our glue crew (our original group of girls we called ourselves the glue crew as we all stuck together) and I was so pleased to see her I punched the air as I came in to the finish… for me this was the finish line and I had come in first with my other girls right behind me… it was a very emotional time with lots of tears and hugs.

Once the realisation set in that we had finished we then cheered everyone else coming in one by one and it was so very lovely, a tremendous achievement for all. Once we were all in, we all stopped for fruit and drink, then we all regrouped and all rode the final 1km to the actual finish line where we all received our medal, champagne and hugs at the entrance to the Ngorongoro crater, it was all very surreal, we had done it, the crew started singing and dancing the usual song and we all joined in like one big party, the pain of the last five days forgotten, we all then text our loved ones to tell them we had done it and then there came a strange feeling of being very lonely, only for a brief moment but I think it was the adrenalin that we had all built up and the sudden realisation that it was over and there was nobody to share it with… A strange feeling but one that we all felt, mixed in with a very proud feeling and wonder at just how on earth we done it but we had. Happy days.

This was one of the hardest things I have ever done in my life but I am so glad I have done it, I have vowed not to do another one… well not for the next year at least!

All back on the buses back down to the lodge for relaxation, dinner and bed, another early start back up the crater for 4am but this time being driven up there in a safari jeep, only this time we are all eager to be up and ready for up the crater for safari, the final day of the challenge and a mixed emotion for everyone but we all had one thing in common - we were doing it alone for ourselves for we each had our own personal reason for doing this challenge, proving something to each and every one of us that we had the strength within us to see it through, and beat our battles, whether they are mental or physical we've got there!

Now for 4 days of relaxation in Zanzibar to digest all that has just happened, all that we have achieved and faced our demons taken a big breath of African air and let all those demons go…

ZANZIBAR

Well, what can I say about Zanzibar other than what a place, sheer paradise. I didn't think a place like that even existed in this world. But it did, and it was here.

I didn't do a diary of my days in Zanzibar because it was a relaxing time, time off from the world but I'll give you an insight into our time in paradise just to tempt you into going yourself and experiencing it in your own way.

The airport to get over to Zanzibar was where it started, and it didn't disappoint. It was a tiny twin-engine plane we were being bundled into. They ushered us six girls into the plane going to Zanzibar and we sat where we could. There was no room to swing a cat! I got a window seat next to a very large African man, so you can imagine, I was squashed up against the window. Lucky enough, I thought the flight wasn't long over to Zanzibar, about half an hour, so I could cope with being squashed.

We took off (bearing in mind the size of the plane). It felt as though the pilot was sitting in an ordinary seat at the front and we were sitting behind him because we could see the instrument panel, etc. A lady came round to give us refreshments, a banana and a bag of nuts (not quite BA standards), and as soon as she gave the food out, we literally dropped out of the sky! It seemed like we had fallen a mile. Probably not that far, but everyone was screaming. The nuts had gone flying, and I sat there without saying a word or moving a muscle. I looked out of the window and thought, Here we go! Flight recovered, and we arrived and departed the airport quicker than anyone could ask us. Welcome to Zanzibar.

We were taken to our paradise room that was going to be ours for the next few days, and it did not disappoint. It was absolute heaven. Our own beach lodges within a luxury hotel complex, with immaculate white sheets on the biggest bed I have ever seen, and it was all mine. No more sharing beds, showers, anything. It was bliss. I collapsed onto the bed and laughed my head off. The sudden realisation of where I was, what I had gone through to get here, who on earth would ever have thought I would end up here... and I was still alive!

A couple of the girls were staying in the same resort, so after some time I unpacked, had a beer, changed into beach clothes, and then went out to find the others. The room looked directly onto the lovely gardens and you could walk down through them to the pool area with music gently chiming in the background; so peaceful and relaxing. I met up with the others. Our drinks were delivered to the pool and our holiday had begun.

It didn't take me and Ali long to get to know where we were and what we could do. We edged our way down to the beach to go looking for shells, but we were ushered back by guards who said it wasn't safe on the beach. I think they expected us to be like the other tourists, but we were having none of it and escaped around the back to get to where we wanted. It didn't take long before a few looky looky guys were trying to sell us some goods, but one of the Maasai guys came and guarded us. He became our island guide and accompanied us everywhere. I think Ali was being set up to marry him, but he wanted to know how many chickens she ate each day and whether he could afford to keep her fed.

He took us along the beach to the huts where the locals set up to sell to the tourists and we became part of their crew. We went into one shack shop run by Coco (as in Coco Chanel) who was trying to sell trousers to some Americans and we ended up doing the deal for her to get her more money. Then we were friends for life and invited to all the places by the locals who thought it was hilarious.

The next day was a trip to Stone Town and Spice Farm, which was amazing. Stone Town was full of sandstone buildings with winding alleys leading to other coral-coloured buildings, all fabulous. Most buildings had seated bars/eating areas on top with a bright coloured sail covering them from the sun. They had big scatter cushions and people smoking shisha pipes. We felt intimidated with so many staring eyes but as long as we stuck together… We found the place where Freddie Mercury was born amongst all the small buildings. The only distinguishing part was the big wooden door to his house. There was little to tell you about the history of who Freddie became. I think I expected a blue plaque or something to commemorate who he was and where he had come from.

We stayed for lunch in an amazing rooftop restaurant where you could see for miles around. It felt like I could stay here all day drinking and eating and relaxing, but onwards bound, we had a spice farm to visit.

Back in the truck, we arrived at the spice farm. It seemed to be deep in the jungle, miles from anywhere. We were introduced to our guide. He was good fun and showed us around, testing our knowledge. We came to some low green spikey bushes and he said, 'What grows here?'

Not one of us came up with the right answer. The answer was pineapple trees. For some reason, I thought pineapples came from palm trees. I never thought they grew from bushes on the ground. Amazing.

Next up, we were walking through a vine that was growing around us and we had to guess again… vanilla pods growing like runner beans. I never knew they grew like this. Then he presented a pod that looked like a green plum, only to split it open and showed us a bright red seed inside. He scraped the red away, which was mace, to reveal nutmeg. You would never know.

We had a complete mind-blowing tour discovering spices and where they come from and what they are used for, our guide spoke little English but he knew certain words and was telling us one spice was used for bang, bang, to which I replied do you mean shagging? He burst out laughing then kept saying shagging and laughing. Later on in the day, when our tour had finished and we were waiting for the truck to go back, I saw the same guide with his next group and how he was telling them this spice was good for shagging; I did giggle, and it made me smile. I had made a difference to his tour!

Zanzibar was full of smiling, dancing, laughing, and joy and I would encourage anyone to visit and experience the true locals. Try to get behind the scenes to see how they live. It will open your eyes, reward you with such a lovely experience and make you realise that money does not buy happiness. The simple things in life are important.

The flight home was made complete when we pulled into Heathrow, loaded our luggage onto trolleys, made our way through customs and out the other side. As I walked along, trying to see if anyone was there to collect me, I saw my son, who leaped through the barriers to run over to hug me. At that moment, I dropped the bags and squeezed with all my heart. I was home.

And yes, I smuggled the shells back home and they proudly live in my bathroom as a constant reminder of just where I have been and how proud I am to achieve what I have done.

Part 5

REFLECTION

Wow, finally picked up this manuscript more than ten years after starting it and I realised I never finished it! I started reading the first page and thought, Wow, that's a good story. Then I realised it was my life, so I had better carry on. Let me take you back to when I had completed Africa; well, a year later.

I loved Cycle Africa so much that I wanted to repeat the experience and the challenge of raising more money for charity. I then joined up for Cycle Vietnam and Cambodia and set about it all over again, doing boot sales, charity disco at the local pub, doing everything to aim towards the final goal, and had the most amazing time raising another £3,000 for women's cancer. This time was different. People had already helped raise funds. They had contributed towards all the evenings quiz nights and everything else. It became a hard old slog to get people to be generous a second time around, especially when you are relying on the same community that helped you previously, so it was more difficult coming up with ideas for fundraising the second time around.

But needless to say, I carried on ploughing through all the different ideas until I reached my target yet again, but it was a genuine struggle and one thing I knew I wouldn't be able to repeat. Not in the least because I didn't have the energy to come up with all these different ideas for raising the money. There was the option of doing the challenge by self-funding, but I knew I would never be able to pay that kind of money myself. Plus, if I wasn't fundraising, it defeated the object of why I was doing it, to raise awareness and rally everyone together to help and there was only so much I could ask the local community to help, so this was looking like it could be my last challenge.

I carried on relentless, more boot sales where my dear old mum would help. She was crammed into my mini full of junk and sitting in the front holding a lampshade whilst balancing a vase on top of her head! (I have some amazing photos of this which raise a smile every time I look at it). I did a London to Brighton bike ride as a training exercise and two Ride the Nights through Central London amongst many other challenges that I completed, raising almost £20,000 in total for Women v Cancer Charity. It truly felt like I had now given back to society for the wrong that I had done in the past and whenever anyone asked me why I did it, I always answered, 'Because I can!'

I intended to do another diary for Cycle Vietnam, but I had burnt myself out because I focused all my energy on the actual challenge. The challenge itself wasn't as hard as in Africa because the landscape was flatter. Not so many hill challenges! We went to some amazing places starting in Vietnam. What a lovely green country, not as poverty-stricken as Africa but a different society, very closed off and not open to the West I felt. I suppose the years of war that they experienced have left the people suspicious of others, or that was my opinion.

The economy was a completely different matter. When I changed my money going into Vietnam, for the princely sum of £38, I got one million Vietnamese Dong that lasted forever and bought so much. We couldn't exchange it when we got to Cambodia, so we had to spend the rest on the last night. I was buying drinks for everyone! Such a difference when we got over to Cambodia. It was a shock to the system to say the least!

We were to cross over into Cambodia via the Mekong River on a four-hour boat trip, something I hadn't even considered until I boarded the boat. Then I remembered I had a bit of a thing about boats and enclosed spaces. We went aboard, but I wasn't even thinking about it and happily followed everyone down into the lower cabin of the boat (which was more like a barge in true Vietnamese style). The girls were taking seats and all I could focus on was the door at the end, which was open. My head started going into mass panic and, before I knew it, I was making a run for the end doors, ready to dive out into the Mekong! The girls knew something was up and started talking to me, calming me down, my head just could not focus on anything other than the open doors. I was crying and panicking, a full-blown panic attack had set in and the only thing that stopped it was one girl sitting with me, talking about everything but where we were. She covered my head with a towel so I couldn't see where I was going. Thank God for Liz and Miffy! This was going to be a long boat trip if I had to do it with my head covered and Liz constantly talking to me, bless her. After an hour or so, I took the towel off and was concentrating on Liz but when we got off, we laughed so much because she had never before talked for four hours non-stop about nonsense.

Crossing over into Cambodia was a completely different market, with lots of corruption and seediness on the streets that we were going through. When you see these countries from a different perspective, not one of a tourist, it really shows the real world and how people survive (or not). You see the tourists being driven in cars just to see the sights, but all they see is what the locals want them to see, not any of the back streets of Siem Reap and all that goes on in them.

At the end of the challenge, we finished at the amazing Angkor Wat, the religious complex of over a thousand buildings built by King Suryavarman II in approximately 1100, some 900 years ago, it is run by Buddhist Monks who practice daily, but when you see them out the back of the buildings having a cigarette, it makes you wonder whether it is all for show.

However, the experience is truly beautiful and a world away from the images of Cambodia. We had the experience of sunrise at Angkor Wat where the sun rose in between the second and third temples and reflected in the lake in front. It was a magnificent sight (despite jostling with so many tourists who each had their camera out on a tripod to get the best view with not a care in the world that it was directly in front of anyone else) and we walked through the ancient relics where the trees have overtaken the ancient remains and wound their way through all the intricate stonework, truly amazing.

We had a few days of free time at the end of the challenge before the flights back home to civilisation and to fit in a few tourist experiences while we were there. I don't think this would be somewhere I would choose to go again.

We experienced the floating village of Tonle Sap. The legend is that in the Cambodian war of the late 70s, the Khmer Rouge, a Communist Political group, forced villagers to flee the threat of poverty and violence. They pushed pallets of wood out onto the water and lived on them, so much so that they built schools on them, houses, restaurants, an orphanage, and even religious structures. The shops sold anything but all at a price. One of the raft boats we visited had a shop with a pit in the middle; there were crocodiles in it and you could pick which one you wanted! The colour of the water extended along the whole river, a kind of muddy grey/brown. The threat of falling out of the boat going there worried me. I wasn't sure if the threat was from drowning or contamination from the water or contents.

We did the usual tourist stuff of visiting the orphaned children and were talked into buying a sack of rice for the children. We thought it would cost a reasonable amount only to find out we were being charged an extortionate price, but it wasn't a situation where you could change your mind. It meant we could only afford one beer on the boat while watching the sunset that night. The locals make a living out of the tourists, but I feel they choose to live that life of poverty on the water; they seem to be happy, as do most people we meet on our travels. It is an eye-opener considering the poverty and filth on the streets.

On another evening we had a different eating experience, a bit like in the jungle on I'm a Celebrity but without the celebrity status, I guess. So, we set off to Bug Café (need I say any more?); the difference was that they were cooked by chefs with spices, etc. Some wonderful memories of us challenging each other to eat the next fried bug (I have a fear of spiders, so to think I ate a crispy one is beyond even me!)

Also, some amazing experiences with incredible ladies that I will never forget, and I am truly thankful that I could take part.

I had put my name down to continue my fundraising challenges with a further trip to India, but I knew this would be a struggle with the fundraising and would definitely be my last one. But India was not to be. I was too busy in my work life for the organisation and my heart wasn't in it anymore. I felt I was pushing myself too far with too little energy for another challenge, so I withdrew from this challenge. Some would say failing to do this challenge, but I certainly did not feel like a failure. I had achieved far more than I had hoped for, and sometimes the lesson is just to be happy with what you have achieved. My lesson was learned. I had given back to society, and I was a better person for it – nothing more and nothing less.

Life for me now is all about finding out who I am and what I want to achieve with my life and all I have learned in it. One of the memorable moments I had back when I was working with a high-end estate agent (not to be named!). I was the property manager, and it was a stressful working environment. I was busy, focused, but I loved it. I needed time out to destress for the sake of my family. One weekend, I packed a bag and took myself off in my car. I thought, Where shall I go? I looked at a map of Cornwall and pulled up a place I had never been to before and decided that was my destination. Approximately five hours later, I pulled into Port Isaac. Because it was my first time, I didn't know to park on the platt. It was full of people, absolutely manic. A guy came over to me and told me I couldn't park there. He took my car keys off me and parked my car somewhere else, never to be seen for the entire weekend. He had introduced himself as Car Park Ken. They were filming Doc Martin (which I had never heard of) so I got myself a pint of Rattler and sat by the side and soaked in the feeling of Port Isaac, a feeling of being at peace and at home with myself, one that would never leave me to this day, and I return as often as I can.

Anyway, I sidetrack. My life had continued in my employment. I had become the best I could be in my chosen path; I had taken on a role to build up the business from nothing, and I had achieved that. As a successful Lettings Manager, I ran a department that was growing every year, albeit the job was stressful, but I had an excellent reputation in the industry.

* * *

My private life had come to a point where no matter how we tried, Mark and I were so bitter we couldn't resolve our situation, so I left and I was fortunate enough to have been offered a derelict cottage from one of my landlords. In return for a reasonable rent, I had to oversee the making good of the property by putting in central heating, rewiring, and decorating. I did it all with pleasure; it felt like home to me, even though I moved in alone, and slept on the wooden floor on a blow-up bed with no heating or curtains on the window. It felt welcoming, like an enormous set of arms hugging me, telling me it will all be okay, just hang on.

My son had stayed in the family home with Mark. Looking back now, it may have been the menopause that made me feel it was the only way to move ahead and start again. When I think back to how my son must have felt, it hurts me. Did he think I abandoned him? Was he torn between me and his dad for loyalty? Who should he go with? I think that this time for him was difficult and led to a period in his life where he didn't know where he belonged and was looking for somewhere he could call home. It's a time I regret very much and wish that we could have resolved things differently for all of us.

After nearly two years apart, which at the time was painful and isolating, and looking back, it was some of the loneliest times I have experienced, but also some of the most soul-searching times which have made me question my actions. They knocked me off my feet and picked me back up again, all in one session.

Sometimes I became obsessed with where my life was going or more about where it wasn't going and where it had all gone wrong. Was I ever to be happy again? Going over and over the damage I had brought to all the family, my children, my relationship, the burden of guilt was overbearing so much so that sometimes I couldn't walk the dog through the woods because I kept looking at the trees weighing up whether a particular branch would take my weight. Desperation drove me to a dark place frequently, but something held me back. When the sun shone, it gave me hope things would get better. I kept saying to myself, It's just a storm. Tomorrow it will be over and the sun will shine. Just hold on tight, pull down the hatch and bury your head till tomorrow. This worked. By the time tomorrow came, I had the energy to push through and hope that with another day, things would become easier. If I kept myself busy on the bad days, I would get through. I painted, I drew, I mended things in the garden; I painted old furniture, anything just to keep busy and take my mind off of what was happening.

I was searching for the next project to do when I had an idea of a kind of sculpture of some degree; I went to the local forge and asked if they could bend me a length of rod iron about five feet tall. They needed a template, so I went and got some cardboard and drew a large curve on it, took it down there and left them with it. A few days later, I called back to collect it, got it home and my dining room became something out of Close Encounters of the Third Kind where the famous Richard Dreyfuss builds his own version of Devil's Tower in his lounge!

I had a large rod of curved iron, filled a garden bucket with Postcrete, and stuck it in the middle. Before I knew it, I had the beginnings of my sculpture. I now had something to focus on and keep my mind busy. I knew what I wanted to create, but wasn't sure how I was going to do it. Starting with what I had, I went from there. Well, that worked out to be lots of garden wire. Then I built a frame. Next, I wondered if doing it with wire meant it would rust, so I searched around for copper wire to wrap around the frame, figuring it wouldn't rust but it would go green, which was okay. After stripping 300 metres of copper wire from electric cabling, it still wasn't finished. I switched to steel to finish some details. It wasn't perfect, but it was to me, so I dug a hole in the garden and put it in the middle of the flowerbed. I had created a silhouette of a naked lady bending over backwards, long flowing hair cascading towards earth, her outstretched arms reaching for the moon or the sun. Welcome to Spirit, my lady of the night looking for peace and sanctuary–it's funny how depression is often relieved by artists who have troubled minds and are looking to keep their minds busy by creating something. Not everyone's cup of tea, but it's not meant to be for everyone, it's for that one person and this was for me. Now every time I walk through the garden, we have a chat and catch up; I have a friend for life in metal form.

It wasn't long after this and approaching Christmas when it soon became clear I was facing life on my own. For whatever reason, the children had all gone their own way and were spending it with their girlfriends/boyfriends' families and I was, for the first time, faced with a Christmas alone. I knew it was going to be a struggle. Rather than put myself through that agony, I signed up to help at Crisis in London, to remind myself that life was tough for lots of people, and I should be thankful. I signed up for three days over Christmas and what a time that was!

On the first day. they put the volunteers in a holding room where they waited to be called to whatever section serving dinners, sorting clothes, bathrooms, cleaning, cooking, creating, music. They had everything covered. It wasn't an overnight place; it was a school or similar that had been let to Crisis over Christmas so they could offer day places where people could go to eat, chat and stay warm. Maybe to have some company over Christmas and play the occasional Christmas Bingo with prizes for the winner. They had thought of everything, with each section catering to every need.

I started in the canteen area, helping people who hadn't eaten for days. There was a system in place to keep everyone safe and no nasty surprises. As the people came in, we offered them a shower and a change of clothes. Over a hot cuppa and some food (tea was endless) then they could chill, do some puzzles, draw, play games, build lego or make something. In addition, they could get help with anything that was troubling them; legal help or just helping them to find somewhere to go or just talk. That was the biggest help anyone could give. Sometimes talking about the family that is no more, either through death, gambling, drugs, drink or choice. Some people didn't want to talk about anything. They wanted to chill without acknowledging there was any issue. Whatever they wanted, it was there.

Because I loved crafting and creating, I moved on to the painting area, helping a few choose what they wanted to create. Going from person to person, I came across a very smart guy, dressed in a suit (but obviously he had been dressed in the same suit for a while) he had a matching bobble hat on and sat quietly painting. He had a pile of pictures in front of him. They were amazing, very abstract but there was something about them that took my breath away. They were so good. The colours he was using gave them a Monet feel, especially the style he was using. So, I sat and talked. He had been coming to the centre for years and also had been on the streets for years, but he was well presented and talked eloquently. He told me drinking had changed his life. He had lost everything and everyone, but he loved to paint. I learned quickly not to question people about what had happened and why; they don't like to be reminded of the past as they can't change it and it hurts to think too much of how their life could be different. So, I listened and only talked when asked. I left him painting, admiring him for all that he had been through. He still kept going. There's a lesson to be learned from him alone.

Next, I went into the entrance hall where they had set up a stage and a karaoke machine. I didn't realise it was karaoke because I thought they were playing music until I saw that the sound I was hearing was coming from one guest; he was singing Nat King Cole's When I Fall in Love. It was so good I stood there with tears in my eyes, amazed at this gorgeous person singing with all his heart. Singing to nobody in particular, but he was in his own world and it was beautiful.

The next person went up and started singing, so I took the hand of an elderly man and asked him for a dance. We danced with tears and smiles. I was so proud to be there. Then another person asked me for a dance and then another. Before long, I had everyone up dancing one by one until the music stopped and the other helpers clapped because they could see the difference it had made by just asking for one dance. The gentleman I was dancing with turned to me and said, 'Thank you for the dance. You have made me feel like a man again.' I told him it was a complete pleasure and I felt so honoured to give them this experience and make them feel wanted and welcomed, even if it was just for an hour.

Then I went on to the canteen and helped serve the food and sat with a few people as they ate. I wanted them to feel like they weren't alone. I don't know who I was helping more, them or myself, I knew for sure it made me feel better and forget all that was going on at home. I was grateful to have a home to go back to.

When the day was almost over, the painter man found me amongst all the people there and gave me something he had done for me, an abstract painting of a lady's face on canvas. I treasure it and it hangs on my wall as a reminder of a time when I saw others with worse troubles than I had. It's a symbol of hope and a reminder to not be complacent. Be thankful for all that you have.

Boxing Day came. That was my last day. Everyone was in a different mood because they knew it was ending and life would soon have to return to normal. We had been warned not to offer accommodation to anyone, pass over contact numbers, or let anyone know where we lived just in case they took our kindness as a weakness and followed us, or worse. I couldn't stay in touch with anyone I had met, but promised to return another year. I drove home to have dinner with my sister and her family and be reminded that it was okay to not be okay sometimes. There is always someone that you can help and make a difference to, just as they will make a difference to you.

* * *

It was New Year's Eve 2018; I had been so low. The relationship I was in was not for me and I had ended it some months before. I had become so focused on where my life was going, but I was bitter that Mark was in a relationship and still living in our home. It was eating me up, thinking of him spending time with our children with his new partner. I seemed to punish myself by putting these thoughts through my head repeatedly. It was not healthy, and I have to keep telling myself to disregard the thoughts until this day,

On the last day of the year, I was going to our local with friends to celebrate and I drove by our old house and walked down the drive. I have no idea why or what I was expecting, but I knocked on the door. I didn't know if Mark would be alone, but I could see him sitting there. He opened the door, and I wished him all the best for the New Year and walked away. I truly meant it. For some reason, all the anger, bitterness, and rage left me. It was then I gave up the fight for our future, our home, and our family and handed it over to fate, no looking back.

Since that day, things got better. I wasn't eaten up with rage or anger. I still missed Mark terribly, but knew it was not to be and I had to accept it. People thought I was mad about giving the house over to Mark and not fighting for my share, but I had no choice. We had destroyed the Deed of Trust all those years ago and now I either had to accept it or it would be held in me as bitterness for years, and life just had to move on.

We had talked to each other without the anger, occasionally going out to breakfast for a catch-up. I could see that life could continue with us both being okay with each other, and all that we had been through, respecting the decisions each of us had made for our own reasons, we still had family and we needed to build bridges for all of us to get over it and move on.

Some months later, Jacob announced he was going travelling to the other side of the world. Mark and I started talking to prepare for our son going on his own. The more we talked, we realised, despite everything, we still had feelings for each other. No matter how hard we tried to put those feelings aside, we couldn't ignore the fact that we cared for each other and we started to see each other again, this time it was out of choice and letting go of all the bad times we had been through. We still felt care for each other and that was a good start, we both felt different and approached the relationship for what it was and not what it represented, we both lived in our separate homes and just took it slowly to see where it led.

The time came for our son to go. He had saved hard and prepared as much as he could. We had no idea how long he was going for or when we would see him again. That was something I couldn't think about. It was too much of a worry. We took him to the airport and stood waving him off, both of us sobbing, the realisation that he had gone. We drove off together and Mark asked if I fancied lunch on the way home, so we stopped off at a country pub and he announced he had a plan. He was going to sell up and go to Cornwall.

My first reaction was, 'I'm gutted, that's where I wanted to be.' I thought he was talking about going with someone else and not me, so I braved it and just said that I wished him well and hoped it all worked out for him until he told me it included me if I wanted to go. I said yes.

The stress started when I had a frantic phone call at five in the morning to say Jacob had landed in USA but they had got the booking wrong and it was the fourth of July, Independence Day and he had nowhere to stay until the following day. Needless to say, I didn't sleep and was worrying so much that he had nowhere to go after a 13-hour flight and a huge backpack. He was on Venice Beach and wandering the streets of America... aaaaaarrrrggghhhh. Phone calls backwards and forwards to the hotel until they agreed to let him stay in the lobby until the next morning. Not the best start, but that's how it was.

Whilst our son was on the other side of the world, we would discuss where he had been and what he was going to do next. When I think about this time, I still can't quite get my head around the fact that our son went to USA on his own, across to Canada, then onto New Zealand with barely enough money at times to even buy himself a meal let alone a ticket home! Luckily for him and us, we had friends in both Canada and New Zealand where he could stay and they took him under their wing which was a godsend, he was only twenty at the time and although some kids of that age seem quite grown up and worldly wise, he was my baby and hadn't been anywhere on his own. But he did it and he survived it. He even survived taking off for a walk on his own down the Grand Canyon despite being advised not to. With only a bottle of water as his companion, dressed in shorts and a t-shirt, he had no way of letting anyone know if he got into trouble! I didn't know about this till after he got back from the Grand Canyon safe and sound.

Jacob was still travelling in New Zealand, when one Saturday I was due to pick up my 84-year-old mum for an appointment. I got out of the shower. Suddenly, I couldn't dry myself. I knew I had to pick my mum up, so I focused on getting dressed, but realised I couldn't put my hands over my head to dry my hair. Looking at the time, my only sense of reason was, 'I need to pick up Mum.' I threw on the clothes at the end of my bed, no underwear so I put on a big chunky wooden necklace that I haven't worn for years (Why? I hear you ask) and walked out the door and tried to get in my car. For what seemed like ten minutes I was trying to get in my car… with no keys! Then I made my way back indoors (I hadn't shut the door) picked up my car keys and promptly got in my car and made my way round to my mum's (it's about a three-minute drive around the block but I cannot remember how I got there). I pulled up and bibbed the car horn. Remember, my hair is dripping wet and I have no underwear on but a big chunky necklace! When my mum got in the car, I went to say, 'Hi sorry I'm late.' It came out complete gobble-de-gook. Luckily, she didn't hear me and carried on chatting but I must have told my brain to be quiet because words were coming out wrong. Somehow that stuck, and I didn't say another word at all, noises like hmm and tut got me by,

Mum realised something was wrong after a while when I wasn't responding, and my driving was becoming erratic. I couldn't determine what side of the road I should be on. After a struggle, (I remember she kept trying to put the car in neutral and I was pushing her hand away to put it in gear) she pulled on my handbrake and flagged down a car to help. The driver was an off-duty policeman I knew. All that I remember is everyone slowly turning up. My sister, my daughter, my brother, my niece, my partner, were all talking to me, not knowing what had happened. Had I taken something? Was I drunk? I could hear them but couldn't answer because I had told my brain to be quiet. I remember when I was sitting there in my car, they were standing around outside the car chatting. I looked up at the sky and thought what a nice day it was. I didn't have a care in the world and didn't know what was going on, where I was or why I was there. It's strange to think I never even thought something had gone wrong somewhere along the line.

The paramedics came, and my daughter and I walked to the ambulance. I remember them asking me some questions and I just kept smiling at my daughter. The paramedics took me away and from that moment I cannot remember getting to the hospital or the next few days. It all became a bit of a blur. My speech was a stutter of simple words, and I couldn't focus on anyone. I could hear and understand everyone but couldn't concentrate on a reply for some days. I was nodding a reply to their questions. My niece and my daughter came in every day and talked to me. Then my son, his partner and Mark came in every night and sat there chatting between them, which helped me. I offered my form of chat, which was a few mixed-up words that made no sense, but they all listened as if my words were coherent. I started speech therapy and walking therapy, which helped to some degree but nothing is better than doing it yourself in your own way. A lot of patience was needed. Those who loved me felt frustrated that they couldn't understand or do more. There are many emotions in place when something like this happens and not everyone understands how difficult it is to communicate, the fact that I am writing this final section of this book two years later is a miracle to be fair as even now my communication is not the best!

I was kept in hospital for two weeks. The doctors were trying to understand what had caused the stroke. My blood and heart readings were fine, I had two clots on my brain and several on my lungs and one side of my carotid artery was completely blocked. But my blood pressure kept dropping and they couldn't understand the reason. The day before I was due to be released pending investigation, my niece was showing me a property she was hoping to buy. She showed me her phone and I remember showing approval and asking where it was. She flicked the screen to the map but suddenly I could see grey blinds being pulled down over my eyes. I couldn't stop them; they were almost down to the floor. Then they stopped but I couldn't see the tops of anything, just a thin bead of light at the bottom of my eyes, which I found hilarious for some reason! I motioned to my daughter that something had happened and I could only see her lips even if I tilted my head back. It was just a strip of light. The doctors rallied around and started testing. It seems I had had another smaller stroke in my brain which had pressed on my retina. The blinds were only temporary and started fading after ten minutes. Then normal service resumed.

My diagnosis was confirmed. I had two brain clots and several in my lungs, which was strange. My cholesterol was okay, my blood pressure was low and for some reason they brought out a heart scan monitor and looked at my heart more closely. It seemed to show blood pumping where it shouldn't be pumping, so more investigation was needed. But, I was released after several days to begin my recuperation at home. It was going to be a long and hard time with many side effects for me and those around me.

* * *

The days at home were slow, with daily visits from therapists who stood over me while I chopped a vegetable to cook for myself. They watched as I went up and down the stairs on my bum and slowly progressed to walking with a handrail that had to be installed as an aid. Mark was visiting every day, my daughter was visiting regularly, and my daughter-in-law was bringing in my beautiful granddaughter to give me hope and force me to play. My sister and my dear mum came in to see me every day to bring me food and make sure I was okay, and Mum was 84! My family was a godsend at this time, and I cannot thank them enough for being there for me, through it all. As for the past ups and downs, none of it mattered anymore as long we had our health, we had everything we needed.

The investigation was followed some months later by a heart test which confirmed I have a hole in my heart and have probably had it since birth, this would have caused the clots and the eventual stroke but why then? Why not when I was cycling up Kilimanjaro? That pushed me to my limit, or indeed why not when I was having twins when my body was pushed to the extreme? It was never picked up. But when the doctor confirmed the results in hospital after I had a procedure where a dye was injected into my veins and then my heart was scanned, I could see clearly on the camera. The blood was pumping out of a large hole at the base of my heart and flowing into the valve where it shouldn't have been. It felt like all my Christmases had come at once; it felt like I had won the lottery. I wanted to jump up and kiss the doctor for finding it; I had a reason this had happened. It wasn't because I had eaten too much ice cream and it wasn't heart disease that had caused the stroke. It was because there was a hole that I didn't know about.

The green light was go for the procedure to correct the hole. They assure me it is non-invasive and will be done through the groin, probably while I am awake with no recovery time needed. I have to wait for the procedure, which may take some months to come around, but as long as I take my blood thinning tablets it's not life-threatening. That's the good news!!! The bad news is that the dreaded pandemic,

Coronavirus, has now hit so all operations have been delayed and the world has become a different place. Lockdown is looming, although that makes no difference to me as I am isolated in my home anyway, work has been impossible, so I depend on sickness benefits to help pay my rent, bills, and shopping. I don't want to be reliant on benefits because of the past. I am paranoid about claiming any benefits, but for this one, I have no option at the moment.

Since the stroke, I find it difficult to concentrate, hold a conversation for any length of time and I have problems staring at a computer screen. Oh, the wonders of modern technology that have made this book possible. I will never cease to be amazed at how far I have come. I will forever be grateful for the chance to survive.

I once tried to go back to my local pub. Obviously, they all knew what happened and welcomed me back with open arms. I walked in there and I was fine talking on a one-to-one basis. I seem to have developed lip-reading skills. When I was listening to someone, I struggled to hear them unless I could see them talking. That was fine when I only had one person to watch. Then someone else joined in the conversation and it became more difficult. Then another person joined us, then another. I left and have never gone back again.

Surgery has now been done and all went well, despite the fact that because of this pandemic I had to attend alone. I was dropped off at the door to the hospital and walked to the ward with my overnight case (which if anyone knows Brighton Hospital, it's a long walk up many stairs, outside and around the corner into another section of the hospital and down another corridor!). I sat in the ward alone, being told to sign a form in case it all goes wrong and then awaiting heart surgery on your own is no fun. Thoughts ran through my head. What would happen if it does go wrong? What if I die on my own with nobody around me, nobody to hold my hand or say goodbye to? It's a harsh reality of this pandemic and one that is so unfair for so many people who have had to lose their loved ones without a goodbye. When you face that situation, there is nothing you can do to change it. No crying will change the situation, no getting angry will change it, so acceptance it is.

Life for me has become very simple and non-dramatic. I reflect on the situation and am at peace with all things. I see everything now for what it is and marvel at nature around me. I am humbled to have sight and tend to sit back, listen to people's stories and take on board all they have been through in their lives. Also, I find I am being asked for my view on things and I offer a non-biased opinion without judging what the person is doing or has done. I give my thoughts as a solution that seems to help resolve their issues without them impacting me personally.

I still struggle with people talking around me. I must concentrate hard on what people are saying because it takes a while for their words to register with me. People don't understand. I need them to talk slowly all the time. They start by doing this but before I know it, I've completely lost what they are saying and just sit there nodding, not joining in the conversation or adding my opinion. I can take it all in but cannot respond in time, so it's better not to respond at all. It's like learning a new language or having a disability, not being able to understand and engage in conversations, but I am learning how to adapt so I can join in by giving one-word answers.

Mark has now sold our family home and decided to move to Cornwall on his own, in the search of our forever home, with the intention of me to follow. Will this be our next step or our ultimate step? Who knows, but for now, Cornwall is calling.

Don't get me wrong, I have aims and ambition and am striving forward with my own goals, but I have learned that there is a time and place for everything and when the time is right, it will be. Force nothing because if it's not meant to be, it won't happen. Let faith guide you and accept things for what they are, not what you want them to be, *c'est la vie* as they say.

Desiderata

by the American writer, Max Ehrmann

Go placidly amid the noise and the haste and remember what peace there may be in silence. As far as possible, without surrender, be on good terms with all persons.

Speak your truth quietly and clearly, and listen to others, even to the dull and the ignorant, they too have their story.

Avoid loud and aggressive persons, they are vexatious to the spirit. If you compare yourself with others, you may become vain or bitter, for always there will be greater and lesser persons than yourself.

Enjoy your achievements as well as your plans, keep interested in your own career, however humble, it is a real possession in the changing fortunes of time.

Exercise caution in your business affairs, for the world is full of trickery, but let this not blind you to what virtue there is, many persons strive for high ideals, and everywhere life is full of heroism.

Be yourself, especially do not feign affection, neither be cynical about love, for in the face of aridity and disenchantment, it is as perennial as the grass.

Take kindly the counsel of the years, gracefully surrendering the things of youth.

Nurture strength of spirit to shield you in sudden misfortune, but do not distress yourself with dark imaginings. Many fears are born of fatigue and loneliness.

Beyond a wholesome discipline, be gentle with yourself, you are a child of the universe no less than the trees and the stars, you have a right to be here.

And whether or not it is clear to you, no doubt the universe is unfolding as it should, therefore be at peace with God, whatever you conceive him to be. And whatever your labours and aspirations, in the noisy confusion of life, keep peace in your soul.

With all its sham, drudgery and broken dreams, it is still a beautiful world, be cheerful, strive to be happy.

The End

Printed in Great Britain
by Amazon

38170453R00138